EQ5 BLOCK BOOK

An Illustrated Guide to the Block Patterns in EQ5

EQ5 BLOCK BOOK

An Illustrated Guide to the Block Patterns in EQ5

The Electric Quilt Company
419 Gould Street, Suite 2
Bowling Green, Ohio 43402

Table of Contents

1 Classic Pieced

1 Classic Pieced

 ## Album (Autograph) Blocks

Album Block

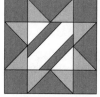

Album-Variable
Star

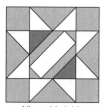

Album-Variable
Star II

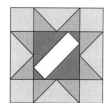

Album-Variable
Star III

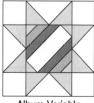

Album-Variable
Star IV

Album-Variable
Star V

Album-Variable
Star VI

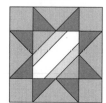

Album-Variable
Star VII

Album-Variable
Star VIII

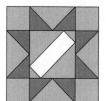

Album-Variable
Star IX

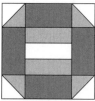

Album-Churn Dash
Variation

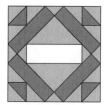

Album Block II

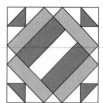

Album Block III

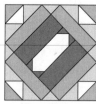

Album Block IV

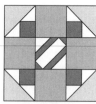

Album Block V

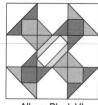

Album Block VI

Album Block VII

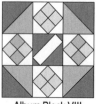

Album Block VIII

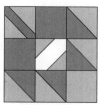

Leaf Album Block

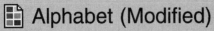
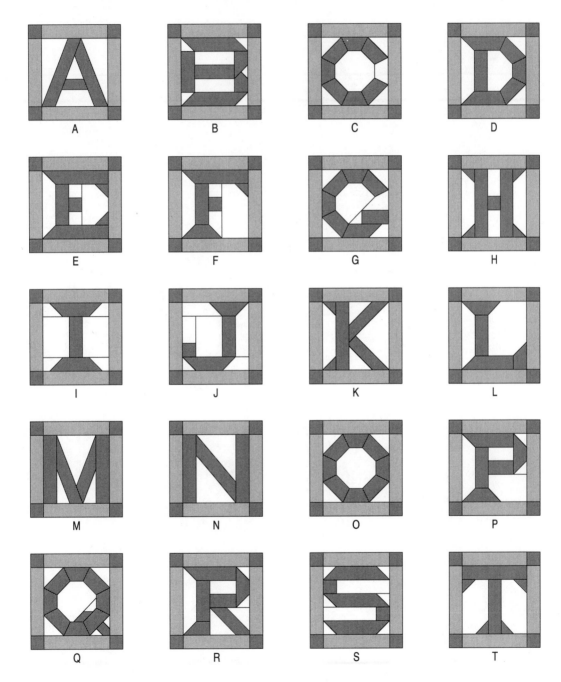

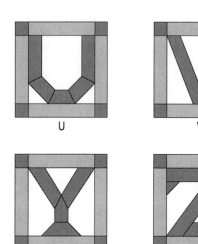
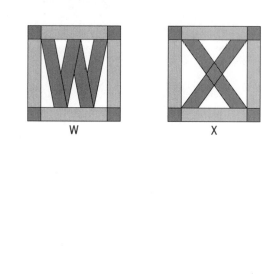

U   V   W   X

Y   Z

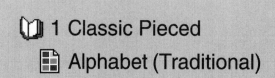

1 Classic Pieced
Alphabet (Traditional)

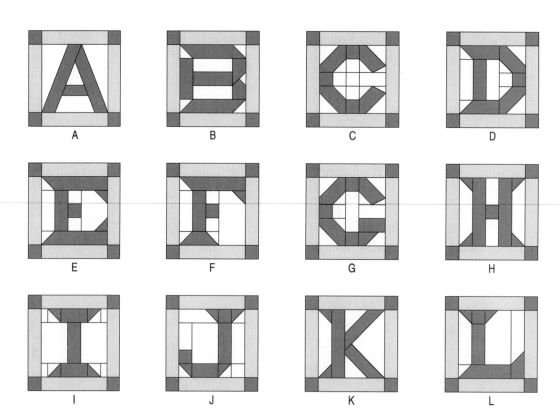

A   B   C   D

E   F   G   H

I   J   K   L

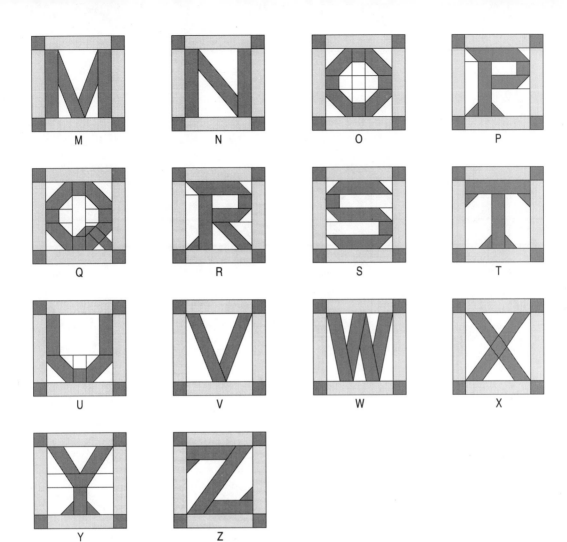

M N O P

Q R S T

U V W X

Y Z

Mosaic, No. 1

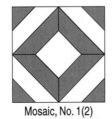

Mosaic, No. 1(2)

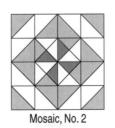

Mosaic, No. 2

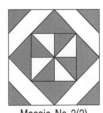

Mosaic, No. 2(2)

Mosaic, No. 3

Mosaic, No.3(2)

Mosaic, No. 4

Mosaic, No. 4(2)

Mosaic, No. 5

Mosaic, No. 5(2)

Mosaic, No. 6

Mosaic, No. 10

Mosaic, No, 10(2)

Mosaic, No. 11

Mosaic, No. 13

Mosaic, No. 13(2)

Mosaic, No. 15

Mosaic, No. 17

Mosaic, No. 18

Mosaic, No. 18(2)

Mosaic, No. 19

Mosaic, No. 20

Mosaic, No. 21

Mosaic, No. 21(2)

Mosaic, No. 22

1 Classic Pieced

 Checked Borders

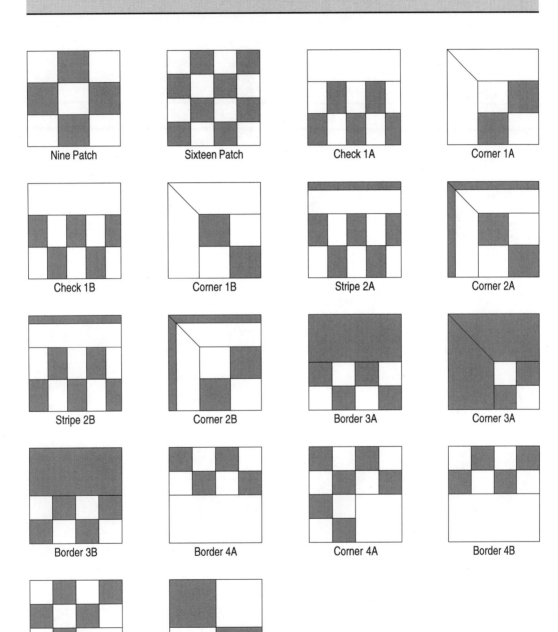

Nine Patch	Sixteen Patch	Check 1A	Corner 1A
Check 1B	Corner 1B	Stripe 2A	Corner 2A
Stripe 2B	Corner 2B	Border 3A	Corner 3A
Border 3B	Border 4A	Corner 4A	Border 4B
Corner 4B	Border 5		

1 Classic Pieced

Classics

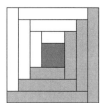

Log Cabin

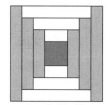

Log Cabin (2)

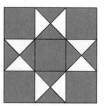

Ohio Star

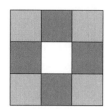

Nine Patch

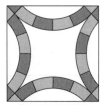

Double Wedding Ring

Quarter Wedding Ring

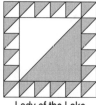

Lady of the Lake

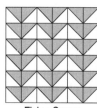

Flying Geese

Bow Tie

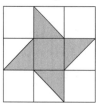

Friendship Star

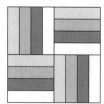

Rail Fence

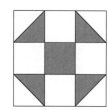

Shoo Fly

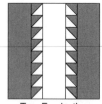

Tree Everlasting

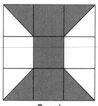

Spool

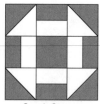

Greek Square

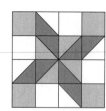

Clay's Choice

Broken Dishes

Birds in the Air

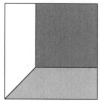

Attic Window

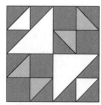

Old Maid's Puzzle

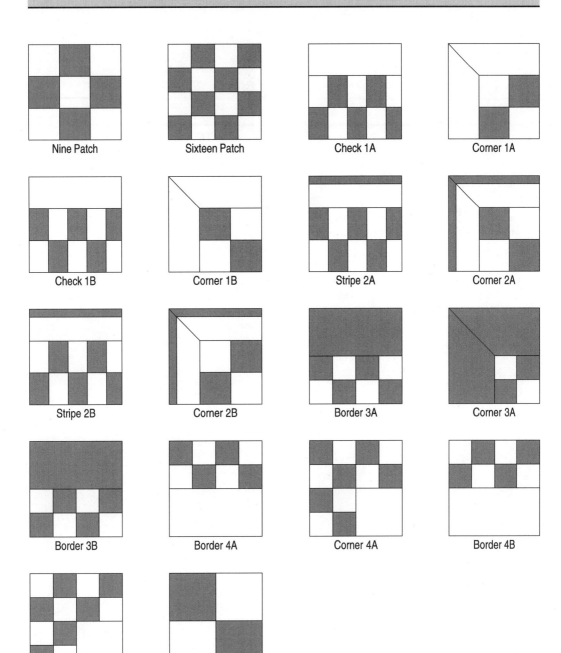

Nine Patch

Sixteen Patch

Check 1A

Corner 1A

Check 1B

Corner 1B

Stripe 2A

Corner 2A

Stripe 2B

Corner 2B

Border 3A

Corner 3A

Border 3B

Border 4A

Corner 4A

Border 4B

Corner 4B

Border 5

1 Classic Pieced

 Classics

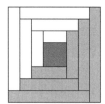

Log Cabin

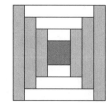

Log Cabin (2)

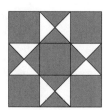

Ohio Star

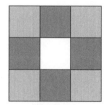

Nine Patch

Double Wedding
Ring

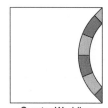

Quarter Wedding
Ring

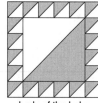

Lady of the Lake

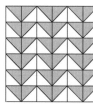

Flying Geese

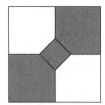

Bow Tie

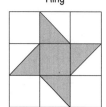

Friendship Star

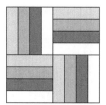

Rail Fence

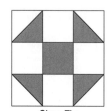

Shoo Fly

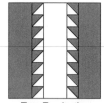

Tree Everlasting

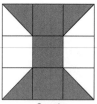

Spool

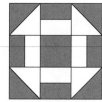

Greek Square

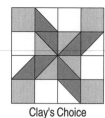

Clay's Choice

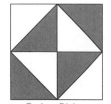

Broken Dishes

Birds in the Air

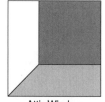

Attic Window

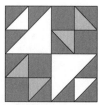

Old Maid's Puzzle

Whirlwind

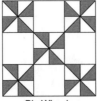

Pin Wheels

Corn and Beans

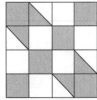

Road to Oklahoma

Cross and Crown

Bear's Paw

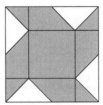

Churn Dash

Indian Hatchets

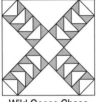

Wild Goose Chase

Monkey Wrench

 1 Classic Pieced

 Compass & Wheels

Compass Star

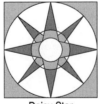

Daisy Star

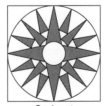

Sunburst

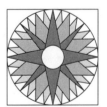

Chips and
Whetstones

Mariner's Compass

Mariner's Compass

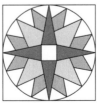

Star Wheel

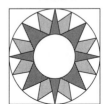

Circle Star

Pinwheel Circle

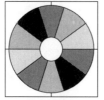

Baby Aster

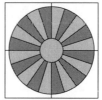

Wheel of Chance

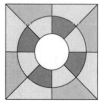

Transparent Circle

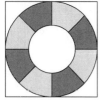

Jelly Donut

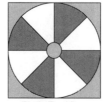

Bird's Eye View

Chariot Wheel

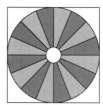

Wagon Wheel

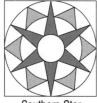

Southern Star

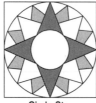

Circle Star

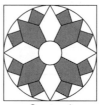

Courtyard

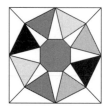

Rising Star

Rising Sun

Round Table

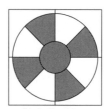

Bird's Eye View

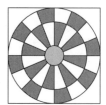

Wheel of Fortune

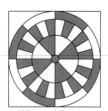

Wheel of Fortune

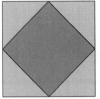

Diamond in the
Square

Economy Patch

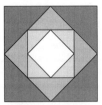

Twelve Triangles

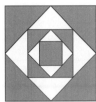

Square in a Square

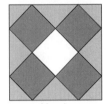

Mosaic

Double Cross

Triple Stripe

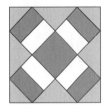

Mother's Dream

Susannah (Variation)

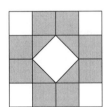

Susannah (Variation)

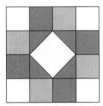

Susannah (Variation)

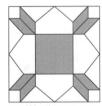

Weathervane

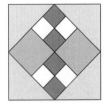

Improved Four Patch

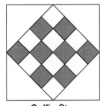

Coffin Star

Grandmother's Cross

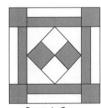

Coxey's Camp

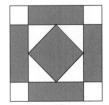

New Album

Art Square

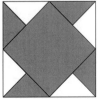

Right and Left

Sugar Bowl

Cross with a Cross

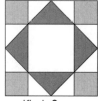
King's Crown

Monkey Wrench

Snail's Trail

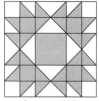
Contrary Wife

1 Classic Pieced
Dresden Fan

3 Petal Dresden
Flower Fan

4 Petal Dresden
Flower Fan

5 Petal Dresden
Flower Fan

6 Petal Dresden
Flower Fan

7 Petal Dresden
Flower Fan

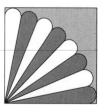
8 Petal Dresden
Flower Fan

3 Petal Dresden Fan

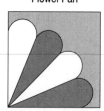
4 Petal Dresden Fan

5 Petal Dresden Fan

6 Petal Dresden Fan

7 Petal Dresden Fan

8 Petal Dresden Fan

3 Petal Small Center
Dresden Fan

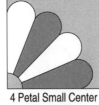

4 Petal Small Center
Dresden Fan

5 Petal Small Center
Dresden Fan

6 Petal Small Center
Dresden Fan

7 Petal Small Center
Dresden Fan

8 Petal Small Center
Dresden Fan

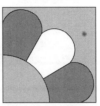

3 Petal Large Center
Dresden Fan

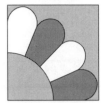

4 Petal Large Center
Dresden Fan

5 Petal Large Center
Dresden Fan

6 Petal Large Center
Dresden Fan

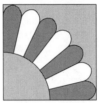

7 Petal Large Center
Dresden Fan

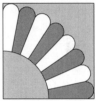

8 Petal Large Center
Dresden Fan

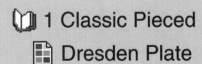

1 Classic Pieced
Dresden Plate

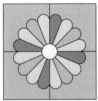

Classic Dresden
Plate

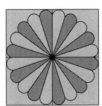

Dresden Flower

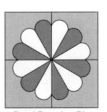

3 Petal Dresden Plate

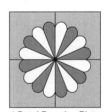

4 Petal Dresden Plate

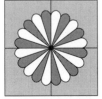

5 Petal Dresden Plate

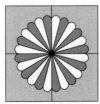

6 Petal Dresden Plate

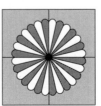

7 Petal Dresden Plate

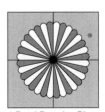

8 Petal Dresden Plate

3 Petal Small Center
Dresden Plate

4 Petal Small Center
Dresden Plate

5 Petal Small Center
Dresden Plate

6 Petal Small Center
Dresden Plate

7 Petal Small Center
Dresden Plate

8 Petal Small Center
Dresden Plate

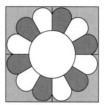

3 Petal Large Center
Dresden Plate

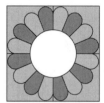

4 Petal Large Center
Dresden Plate

5 Petal Large Center
Dresden Plate

6 Petal Large Center
Dresden Plate

7 Petal Large Center
Dresden Plate

8 Petal Large Center
Dresden Plate

1 Classic Pieced
Drunkard's Path

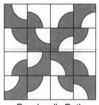

Drunkard's Path

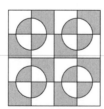

Indiana Puzzle

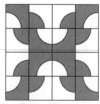

Falling Timbers

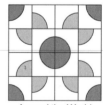

Around the World

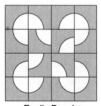

Fool's Puzzle

Drunkard's Path

Drunkard's Path

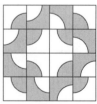

Dove

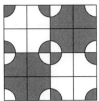

Millwheel

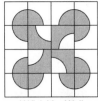

I Wish You Well

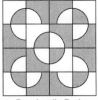

Drunkard's Path
Variation I

Steeplechase

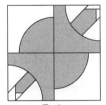

Turtle

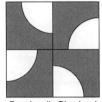

Drunkard's Pinwheel

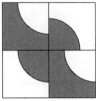

Peace Dove

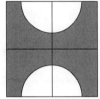

Over the Bridge

Around the World

Baseball

 1 Classic Pieced
 Eccentrics

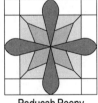

Paducah Peony

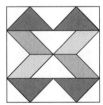

Ribbons

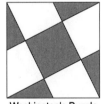

Washington's Puzzle

Slashed Album

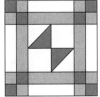

Odds and Ends

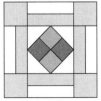

Coxey's Camp

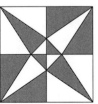

Crossed Canoes

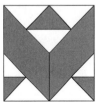

Ribbon Border

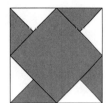

Right and Left

Work Box

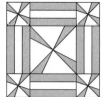

Tangled Lines

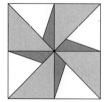

Double Pinwheel
Whirls

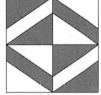

Left and Right

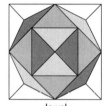

Jewel

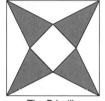

The Priscilla

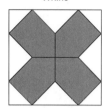

The Mayflower

1 Classic Pieced
Eight-Point Stars

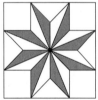

Star of the East

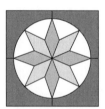

Royal Diamonds

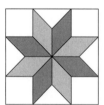

Diamond

Blazing Star

Love in a Mist

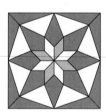

Pole Star

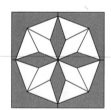

Octagon Star

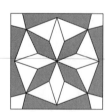

Octagon Star

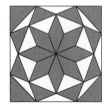

Western Spy

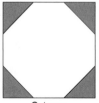

Octagon

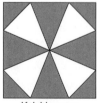

Kaleidoscope

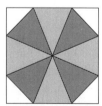

Kaleidoscope (2)

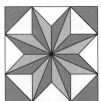

Silver and Gold

Eight-pointed Star

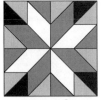

Lemoyne Star
Variation

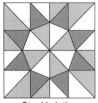

Star Variation

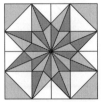

St. Louis Star (Adap.)

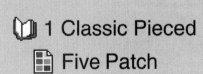

1 Classic Pieced
Five Patch

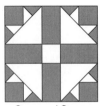

Cross and Crown

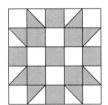

Four X Star

Goose Tracks

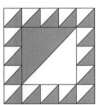

Lady of the Lake

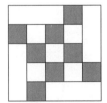

Flying Squares

Square and a Half

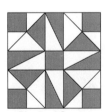

Pinwheel Square

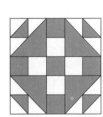

Duck and Ducklings

Handy Andy

Bird's Nest

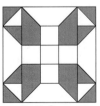

Fool's Square

St. Louis Star

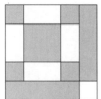

Children's Delight

King's Crown

Red Cross

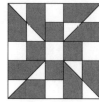

Crazy House

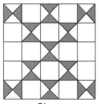

Clown

Providence Quilt
Block

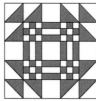

Goose in the Pond

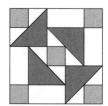

Grandmother's
Puzzle

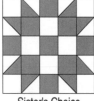

Sister's Choice

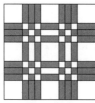

Album Quilt

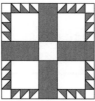

Premium Star

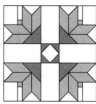

Fanny's Fan

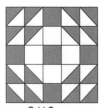

Odd Scraps
Patchwork

 1 Classic Pieced

 Four Patch

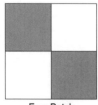

Four Patch

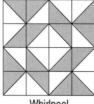

Whirlpool

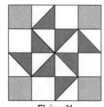

Flying-X

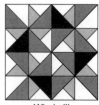

Windmill

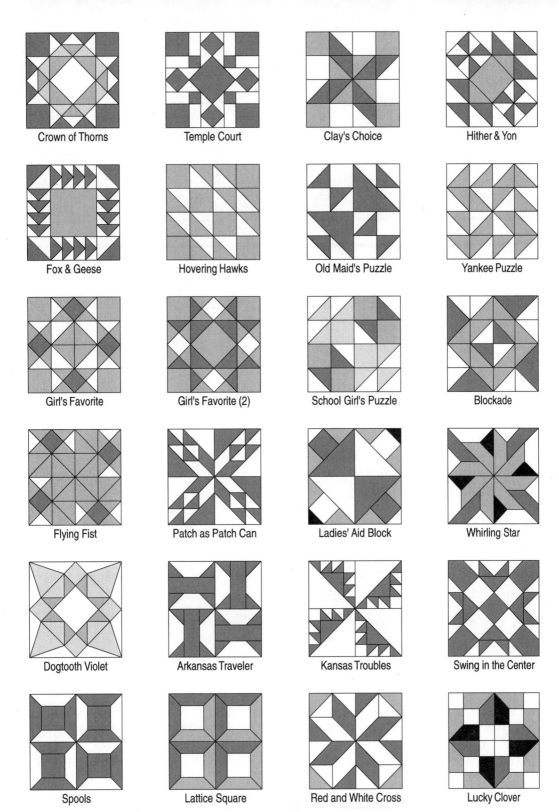

Crown of Thorns

Temple Court

Clay's Choice

Hither & Yon

Fox & Geese

Hovering Hawks

Old Maid's Puzzle

Yankee Puzzle

Girl's Favorite

Girl's Favorite (2)

School Girl's Puzzle

Blockade

Flying Fist

Patch as Patch Can

Ladies' Aid Block

Whirling Star

Dogtooth Violet

Arkansas Traveler

Kansas Troubles

Swing in the Center

Spools

Lattice Square

Red and White Cross

Lucky Clover

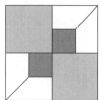

Four-Patch Variation

Blue Boutonnieres

Carrie Nation Quilt

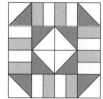

Cross Roads

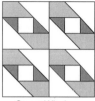

Garret Windows

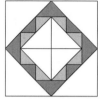

Vines at the Window

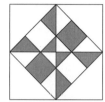

Storm Signal

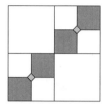

Dad's Bow Tie

Dutchman's Puzzle

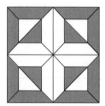

White Cross

Star and Cubes

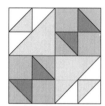

School Girl's Puzzle

 1 Classic Pieced

 Ladies Art Company

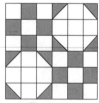

Flagstones

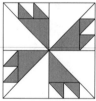

Rosebud

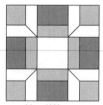

Hand Weave

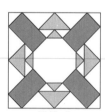

All Kinds

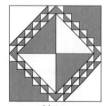

Linton

Roman Cross

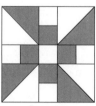

Propeller

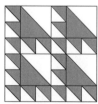

Lost Ship Pattern

Texas Flower	Cross within Cross	Widower's Choice	Bird's Nest
Merry Kite	Star of North Carolina	Navajo	Baton Rouge Block
Santa Fe Block	Magic Circle	Album	Double Z
Storm at Sea	Chicago Star	Devil's Puzzle	Star and Chains
World's Fair Puzzle	New Star	Wheel of Fortune	Crosses and Star
Bat's Wings	Cut Glass Dish	DoubleX, No.1	DoubleX, No.2

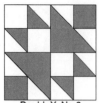

DoubleX, No.3

DoubleX, No.4

Capital T

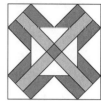

Texas Tears

Old Maid's Ramble

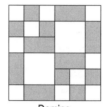

Domino

Letter H

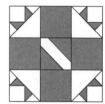

W.C.T. Union

Leap Frog

Steps to the Altar

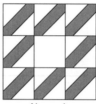

Nonsuch

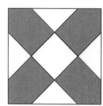

A Snowflake

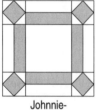

Johnnie-
Round-the-Corner

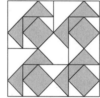

T Quartette

 1 Classic Pieced

 Nine Patch

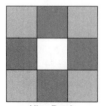

Nine Patch

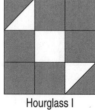

Hourglass I

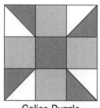

Calico Puzzle

Attic Window

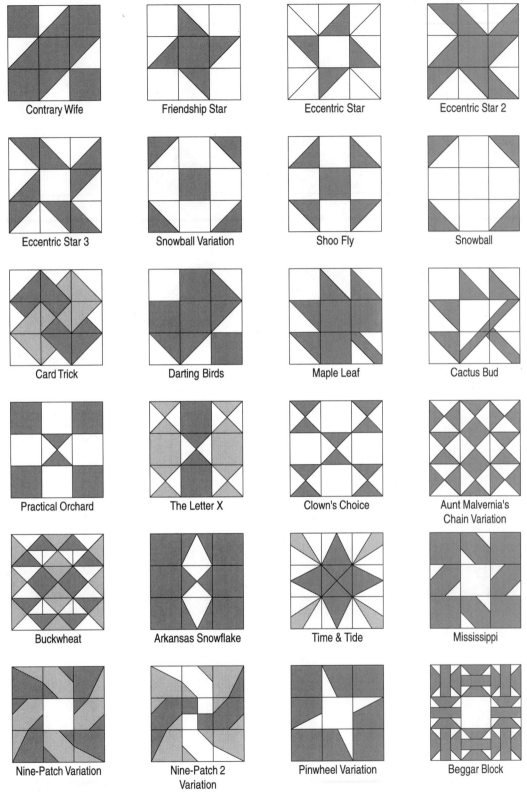

Contrary Wife

Friendship Star

Eccentric Star

Eccentric Star 2

Eccentric Star 3

Snowball Variation

Shoo Fly

Snowball

Card Trick

Darting Birds

Maple Leaf

Cactus Bud

Practical Orchard

The Letter X

Clown's Choice

Aunt Malvernia's
Chain Variation

Buckwheat

Arkansas Snowflake

Time & Tide

Mississippi

Nine-Patch Variation

Nine-Patch 2
Variation

Pinwheel Variation

Beggar Block

Optical Illusion

Letter X

Arkansas Snowflake

Cats and Mice

Rolling Stone

Broken Wheel

Road to California

Rolling Squares

Kansas Star

Arbor Window

Storm Signal

All Hallows

Wyoming Valley

Bird of Paradise

Stellie

Mollie's Choice

Joseph's Coat

Summer Winds

Double Monkey
Wrench

Grecian Square

Greek Cross

Aunt Dinah

Shoo Fly

Saw Tooth

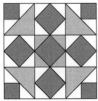

Five Spot

The Windmill

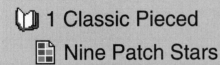

1 Classic Pieced
Nine Patch Stars

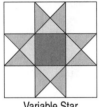

Variable Star

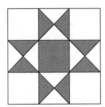

Aunt Eliza's Star

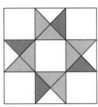

Twin Star

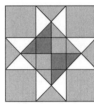

Country Farm

Star Variation

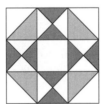

Swamp Angel

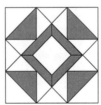

Card Basket

Ornate Star

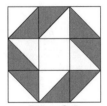

Ribbon Quilt

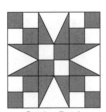

Garden Patch

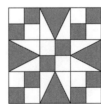

Fifty-Four-Forty-or-Fight

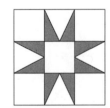

Eight-pointed Star

Old Snowflake

Nine Patch Star

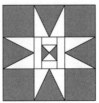

Dove at the Window

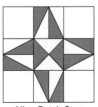

Nine Patch Star

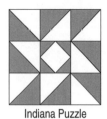

Indiana Puzzle

📖 1 Classic Pieced
📄 Old Favorites

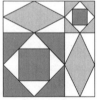

Storm at Sea

Chinese Lanterns

Pieced Bouquet

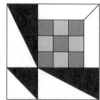

Nose-Gay

Silver Maple

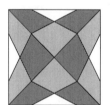

Jewel Star

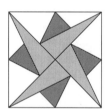

Starry Path

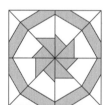

Road to Fortune

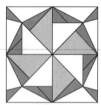

Lucky Star

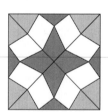

Full Blown Tulip

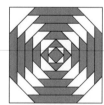

Pineapple

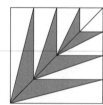

The Palm

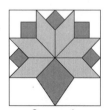

Cornucopia

Lotus Block

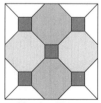

Meadow Flower

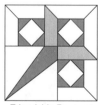

Friendship Bouquet

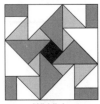

Whirligig

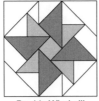

Double Windmill

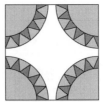

Setting Sun

 1 Classic Pieced
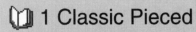 Orange Peels Etc.

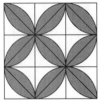

Orange Peel Variation

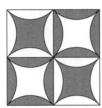

Sugar Bowl

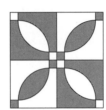

True Lover's Knot

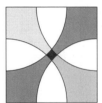

Flowering Snowball

Papa's Delight

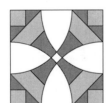

Raleigh

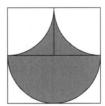

Clamshell

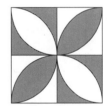

Flower Petals

Joseph's Coat

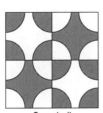

Snowball

Melon Patch

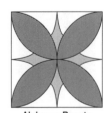

Alabama Beauty

Grist Mill

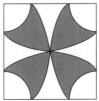

Four Leaf Clover

Friendship Circle

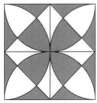

Spring Beauty

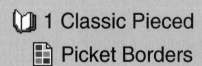
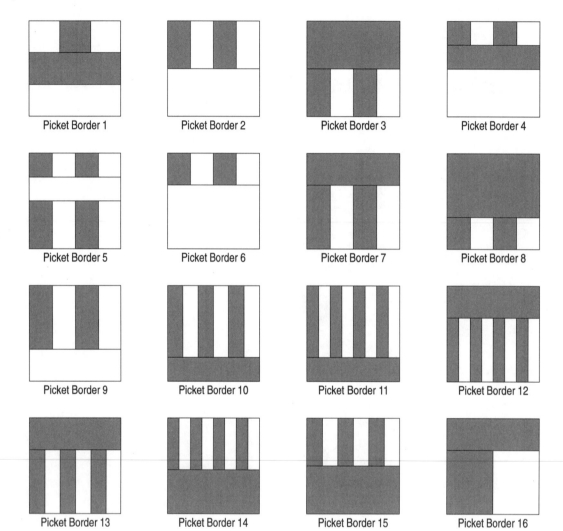

Picket Border 1   Picket Border 2   Picket Border 3   Picket Border 4

Picket Border 5   Picket Border 6   Picket Border 7   Picket Border 8

Picket Border 9   Picket Border 10   Picket Border 11   Picket Border 12

Picket Border 13   Picket Border 14   Picket Border 15   Picket Border 16

1 Classic Pieced

 ## Pictures

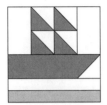

Sailboat Quilt

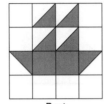

Boat

Airways

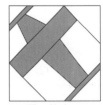

The Airplane

Jack's House

The Old Homestead

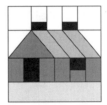

House on the Hill

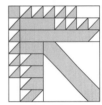

Proud Pine

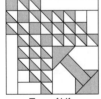

Tree of Life

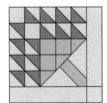

Pine Tree

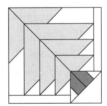

Pine Tree Quilt

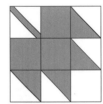

Maple Leaf

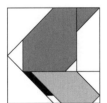

The Butterfly Quilt (2)

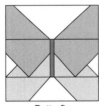

Butterfly

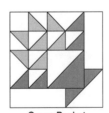

Grape Basket

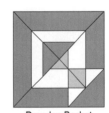

Dresden Basket

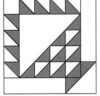

Basket Quilt in
Triangles

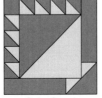

Cake Stand

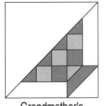

Grandmother's
Basket

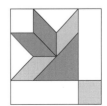

Flower Pot

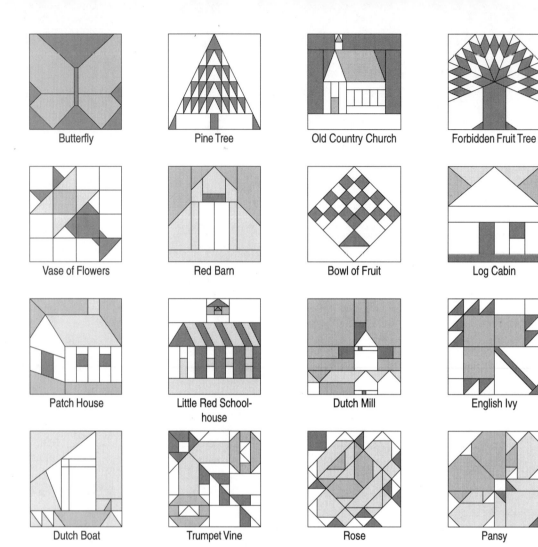

Butterfly

Pine Tree

Old Country Church

Forbidden Fruit Tree

Vase of Flowers

Red Barn

Bowl of Fruit

Log Cabin

Patch House

Little Red School-
house

Dutch Mill

English Ivy

Dutch Boat

Trumpet Vine

Rose

Pansy

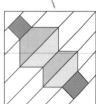

Lantern

Fruit Basket

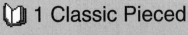

Half-Square Triangle

Half-Square
Triangle 2

Diagonal Strips

Diagonal Strips 2

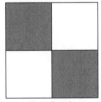

Four Patch

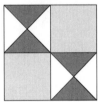

Four-Patch Variation

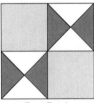

Four-Patch
Variation 2

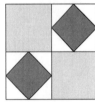

Four-Patch
Variation 3

Indian Hatchets

Indian Hatchets 2

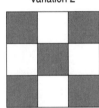

Nine Patch

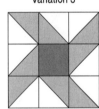

Eccentric Star

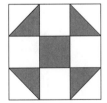

Shoo Fly

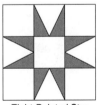

Eight-Pointed Star

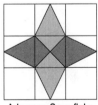

Arkansas Snowflake

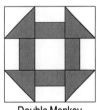

Double Monkey
Wrench

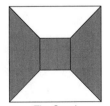

The Spool

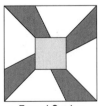

Formal Garden
Variation

World Without End
Variation

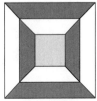

Box-in-a-Box
Variation

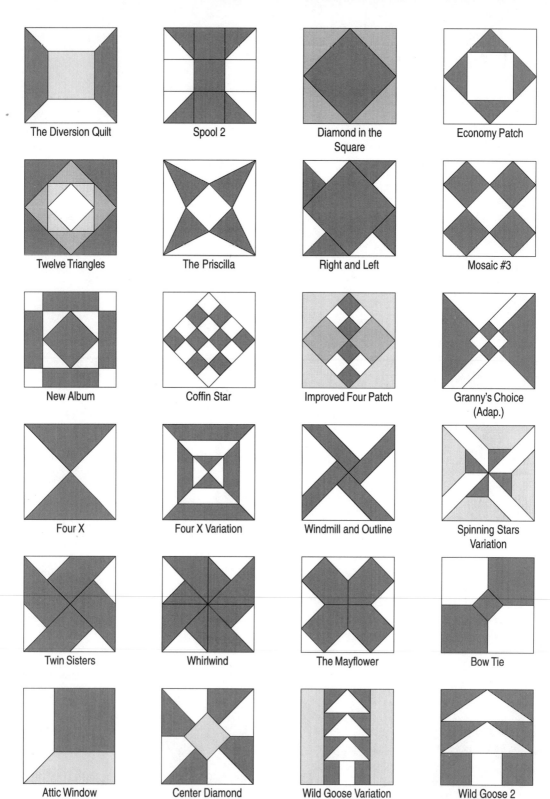

The Diversion Quilt

Spool 2

Diamond in the Square

Economy Patch

Twelve Triangles

The Priscilla

Right and Left

Mosaic #3

New Album

Coffin Star

Improved Four Patch

Granny's Choice (Adap.)

Four X

Four X Variation

Windmill and Outline

Spinning Stars Variation

Twin Sisters

Whirlwind

The Mayflower

Bow Tie

Attic Window

Center Diamond Variation

Wild Goose Variation

Wild Goose 2 Variation

Wild Goose Chase

Wild Goose Chase

Wild Goose Chase

Wild Goose Chase

 1 Classic Pieced
 Stars

Square and a Half

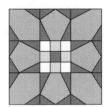

Klondike Star

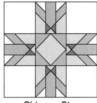

Chicago Star

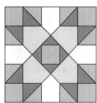

Providence Quilt Block

Uncle Sam's Hourglass

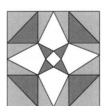

Little Rock Block

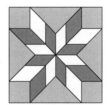

Star Variation

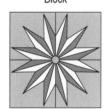

Split 12 Point Star

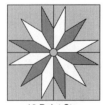

12 Point Star

Flower Star

Rolling Plate

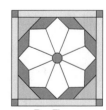

Fan Flower

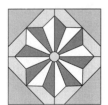

Purple Coneflower

Sunbeam

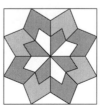

Double Star

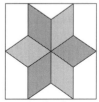

Morning Star

1 Classic Pieced
Striped Borders

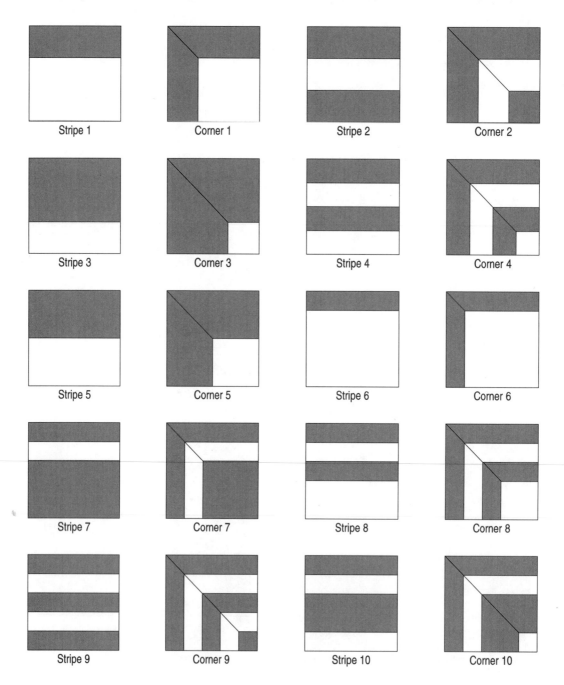

Stripe 1	Corner 1	Stripe 2	Corner 2
Stripe 3	Corner 3	Stripe 4	Corner 4
Stripe 5	Corner 5	Stripe 6	Corner 6
Stripe 7	Corner 7	Stripe 8	Corner 8
Stripe 9	Corner 9	Stripe 10	Corner 10

Stripe 11

Corner 11

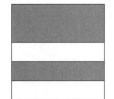

Stripe 12

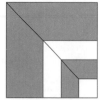

Corner 12

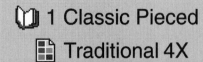

📖 1 Classic Pieced
📑 Traditional 4X

Basic 4X

Checkerboard

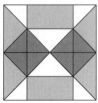

Boise

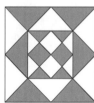

Cock's Comb

Aunt Melvernia's
Chain

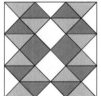

Buckwheat

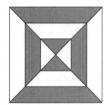

Four X Variation

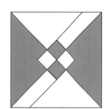

Granny's Choice
(Adap.)

The Arrowhead

Sarah's Favorite

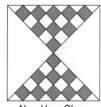

New Hour Glass

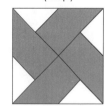

Twin Sisters

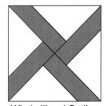

Windmill and Outline

Criss Cross Variation

Criss Cross Variation

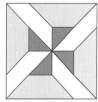

Spinning Stars
Variation

Good Luck

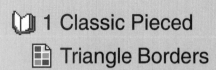

📖 1 Classic Pieced

📄 Triangle Borders

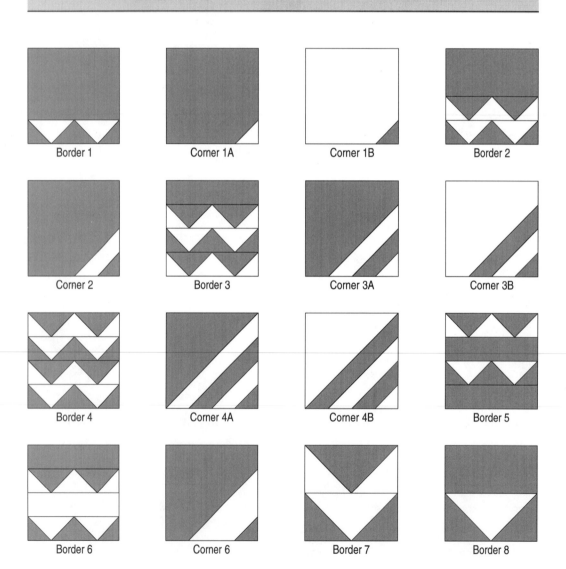

Border 1   Corner 1A   Corner 1B   Border 2

Corner 2   Border 3   Corner 3A   Corner 3B

Border 4   Corner 4A   Corner 4B   Border 5

Border 6   Corner 6   Border 7   Border 8

Corner 8A

Corner 8B

Border 9

Sawtooth Border 1

Double Sawtooth

Wild Goose Chase Border

Diamond Border

Diamond Border 2

Check and Triangle Border

Check and Triangle 2

Check and Triangle 3

Check and Triangle 4

Stripe and Strips

Stripe and Strips II

Stripe and Strips III

Triangles and Strips

Triangles and Strips 2

Triangles and Strips 3

Diamonds and Strips

Geese and Strips

Meeting Geese & Strips

Geese and Strips 2

Chevrons & Strips

Slanting Stripes & Strips

Triple Slanting Strips

Zig Zags

Triple Triangles

Double Diamonds

Meeting Double
Diamonds

Triangles

Meeting Triangles

Diamond in Square
Strips

Chevrons and Stripes

Meeting Chevrons

More Diamonds &
Strips

Double Diamonds 2

Diamonds & Triangles

Up and Down
Triangles

Tree Everlasting
Border

Tree Everlasting 2

Zig Zag 2

Zig Zag 3

Zig Zag 4

Zig Zag 5

2 Contemporary Pieced

January Autograph

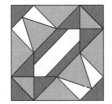

February Autograph

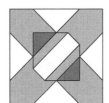

March Autograph

April Autograph

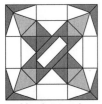

May Autograph

June Autograph

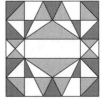

July Autograph

August Autograph

September Autograph

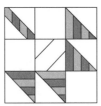

October Autograph

November Autograph

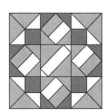

December Autograph

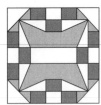

Monday Autograph

Tuesday Autograph

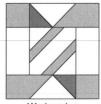

Wednesday
Autograph

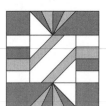

Thursday Autograph

Easter Basket

Topiary

Barbershop Baskets

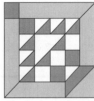

Checkerboard Basket

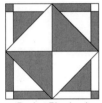

Basket Pinwheel

Postmodern Basket

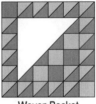

Woven Basket

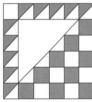

Berry Basket

Scrap Basket

Sun & Shadow
Basket

Lily Basket

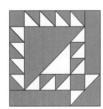

Amish Basket

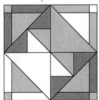

Sun & Shadow
Baskets

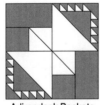

Adirondack Baskets

Sugar Creek Basket

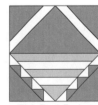

Rick-Rack Basket

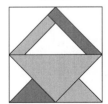

Brittany Basket

Log Cabin Basket

Charm Basket

Nine-patch Baskets

Megan's Baskets

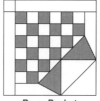
Berry Basket

Double-Baskets

Rick-Rack Basket

  2 Contemporary Pieced
Cross Variations

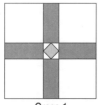
Cross 1

Cross 2

Cross 3

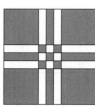
Cross 4

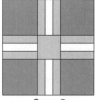
Cross 5

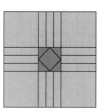
Cross 6

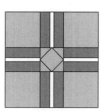
Cross 7

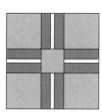
Cross 8

Cross 9

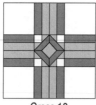
Cross 10

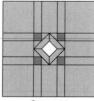
Cross 11

Cross 12

Cross 13

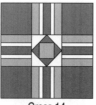
Cross 14

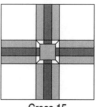
Cross 15

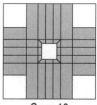
Cross 16

2 Contemporary Pieced

Fans

Fanblades

Rainbow Fan

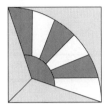

Floating Fan

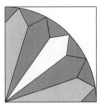

Tie Fan

Diamond Diane's Fan

Leaf Fan

North Baltimore Fan

Louvre Fan

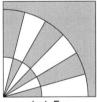

Jan's Fan

Petal Fan

Daisy Petal Fan

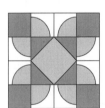

Fan Flower

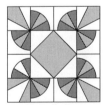

Butterfly Fan

Fan Dance

Fat Quarters Fan

Silk Rainbow

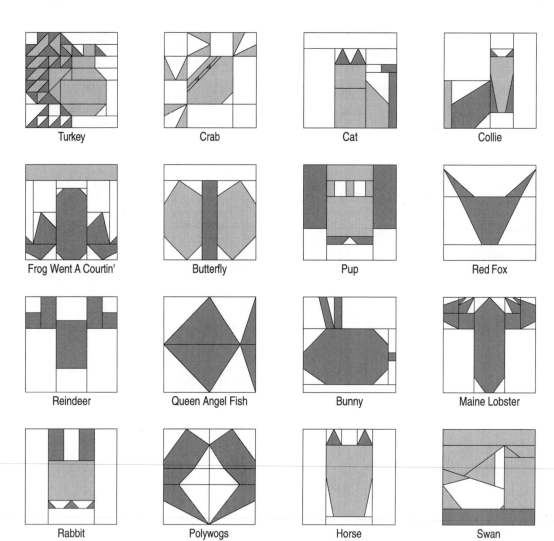

Turkey

Crab

Cat

Collie

Frog Went A Courtin'

Butterfly

Pup

Red Fox

Reindeer

Queen Angel Fish

Bunny

Maine Lobster

Rabbit

Polywogs

Horse

Swan

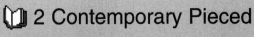
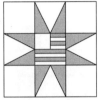

Eight-Point Flag

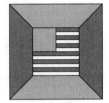

Flag in a Box

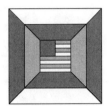

Flag in a Box II

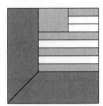

Attic Flag

Flag in the Square

Wild Goose Flag

Wild Goose Flag II

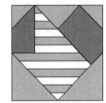

Heart Flag

Heart Flag II

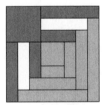

Log Cabin Flag

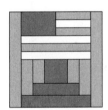

Log Cabin Flag II

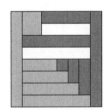

Log Cabin Flag III

Lady of the Lake Flag

Whirlwind Flag

Rail Fence Flag

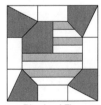

Pinwheel Flag

2 Contemporary Pieced
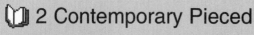

Buds and Ribbons

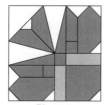

Blossom

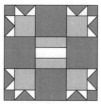

Sunflower

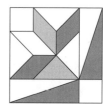

Peony

Amaryllis Bulb

Picnic Bouquet

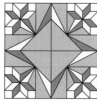

Daffodil Ring

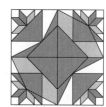

Alpine Flower

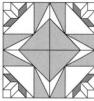

Floral Wreath

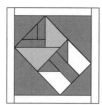

Rosebud

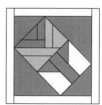

Rose

Foxglove

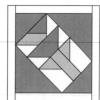

Foxglove Too

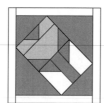

Tulip

Lily Block

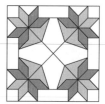

Lily Wreath

9-patch Snowball

4-patch Snowball

Rail Fence Quilt

9-patch

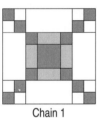

Chain 1

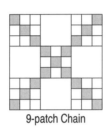

9-patch Chain

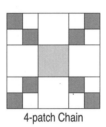

4-patch Chain

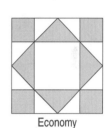

Economy

Economy II

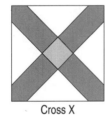

Cross X

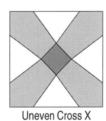

Uneven Cross X

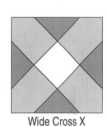

Wide Cross X

Broken Sash Strip

Broken Sash Strip II

Broken Sash Strip III

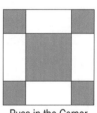

Puss in the Corner

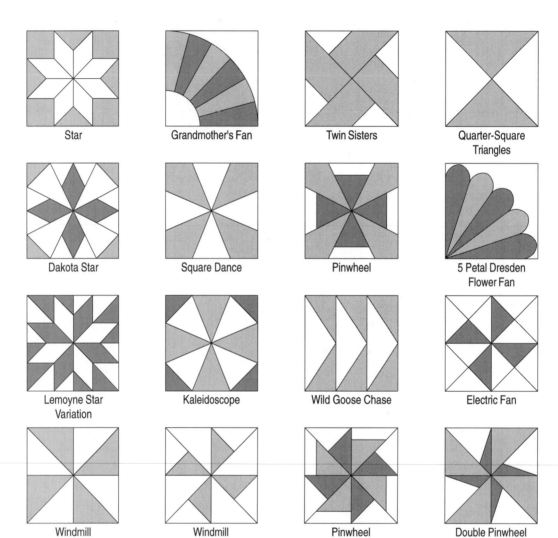

Star

Grandmother's Fan

Twin Sisters

Quarter-Square Triangles

Dakota Star

Square Dance

Pinwheel

5 Petal Dresden Flower Fan

Lemoyne Star Variation

Kaleidoscope

Wild Goose Chase

Electric Fan

Windmill

Windmill

Pinwheel

Double Pinwheel Whirls

Home Delights

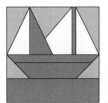

Bathtub Boat

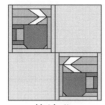

Hot Latte

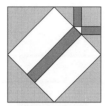

Birthday Party

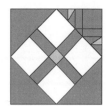

Happy Returns

Bird House

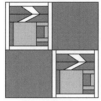

Good Morning

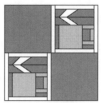

Good Night

He

She

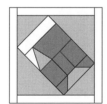

Toy Barn

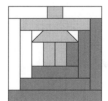

Log Cabin Doll

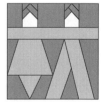

She and He by Judy
Vigiletti

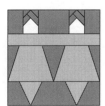

Two Friends by Judy
Vigiletti

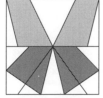

Butterfly by Judy
Vigiletti

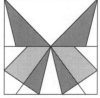

Butterfly Too by Judy
Vigiletti

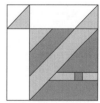

Fish by Judy Vigiletti

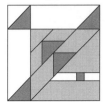

Fish Too by Judy
Vigiletti

Fish Too II by Judy
Vigiletti

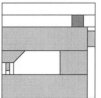

Sewing Machine

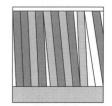

Fabric Bolts

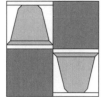
Thimbles

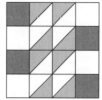
EQ Logo

Star of David (Debbie Sichel)

Star of David 2 (Debbie Sichel)

Star of David 3 (Debbie Sichel)

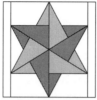
Star of David 4 (Debbie Sichel)

  2 Contemporary Pieced Houses

Brooklyn

St. Louis

Chicago

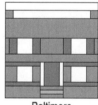
Baltimore

Milwaukee

Philadelphia

Detroit

Kansas City

Saltbox

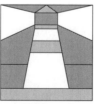
Lighthouse

Prairie House

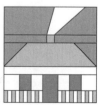
Picket Fence

Terrie's in Taos

Condo

Wisconsin Cabin

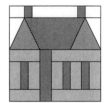

The Lake Cottage

Old Two-Story

Ann's House

Country Cottage

  2 Contemporary Pieced
Kaleidoscopes

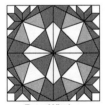

Rose Window

Diamond Bracelet

Dunce Caps

Alpine Flower

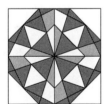

Electric Fan

Puzzle Ball

Pinball Swirl

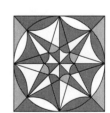

Faceted Star

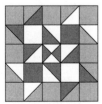

Modern Milky Way

Comet

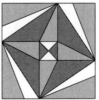

Jupiter

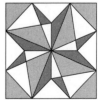

Cat's Tails

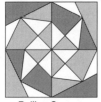

Rolling Crosses

Diamond Ring

Lobster Claws

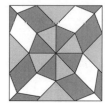

Gemstone

2 Contemporary Pieced
Log Cabin-Like

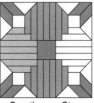

Courthouse Stars

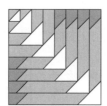

Rotary Ribbon

Strip Circles

Fan Rails

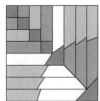

Round Cabin

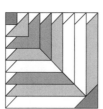

Scrappy Stripper

Rainbow Logs

Starflower

Interlaced Logs

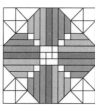

Irish Logs

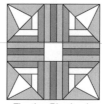

Floating Pinwheels

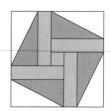

Lacy Lattice Work

Striped Lattice Work

3's

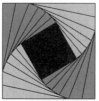

7's

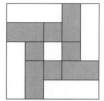

High Flying Squares

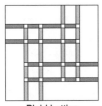
Plaid Lattice

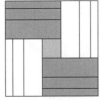
Woven Logs

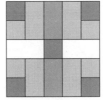
Plaid Fab

 2 Contemporary Pieced

 New Stars

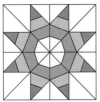
String Star

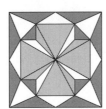
Hopatcong Star

Shadow Star

Sedona Star

Mule Shoe TX

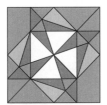
Bettina's Star

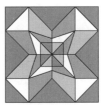
Cheyenne Star

Folded Star

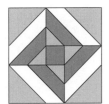
Strip Star

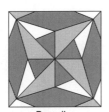
Propeller

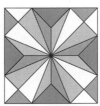
Savannah Star

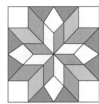
EQ's Stars & Beams

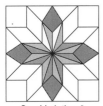
Star Variation 2

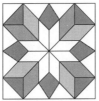
Star Variation 3

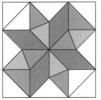
EQ Star

EQ Star 2

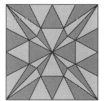

EQ Star 3

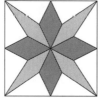

EQ Star 4

EQ Star 5

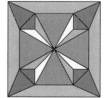

EQ Star 6

EQ Kaleidoscope
Star

 2 Contemporary Pieced

 Pinwheels & Potpourri

Woven Lattice

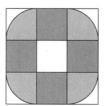

Button

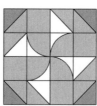

Electric Fan

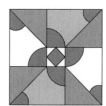

Scrap Blossoms

Fan Weaver

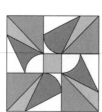

Windmill

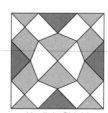

Ucello's Shield

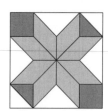

Costume Jewelry

Opening Gates

Belt Buckle

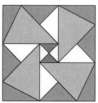

Origami

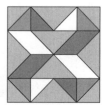

Walking X

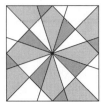
Spinning Blades

Shining Bright

Jungle Flower

Cool Fan

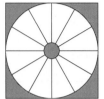
One Wheel with 12 Spokes

Three Wheels with 12 Spokes

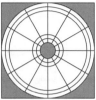
Five Wheels with 12 Spokes

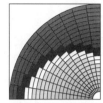
Nine Degree Wedge

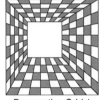
Perspective Grid 1

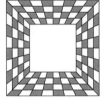
Perspective Grid 2

 2 Contemporary Pieced

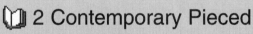 Prairie Style

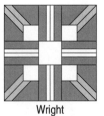
Wright

Stickley

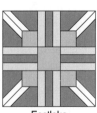
Eastlake

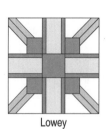
Lowey

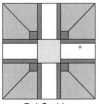
Downing

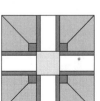
Bel Geddes

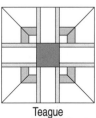
Teague

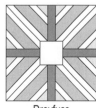
Dreyfuss

Sullivan

Burnham

Fuller

Gropius

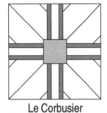
Le Corbusier

Bradley

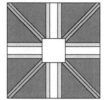
Roycroft

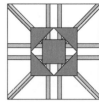
Fargo

 2 Contemporary Pieced

 Royal Crowns

Old Snowflake

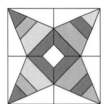
Whirligig

Country Crown

Meadow Flower

String Star

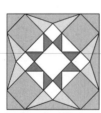
Crossing Winds

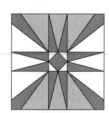
Tall Star

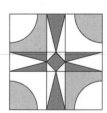
Jack of Diamonds

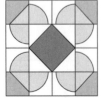
Scrap Violet

Galaxy

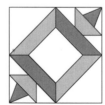
Rotate Me

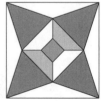
3-D

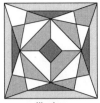

Illusion

Metalwork

Metalwork Variation

Metalwork Variation II

 2 Contemporary Pieced
Secondary Surprises

Trading Post

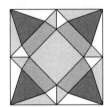

Harlequin

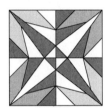

Jungle Star

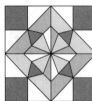

Windmill

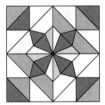

Windmill II

Fireworks

Scrap Sparkler

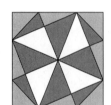

Tumbling Cube

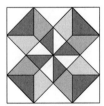

Checked X

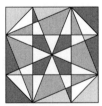

Emerging Star

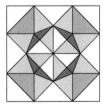

Faceted Star

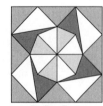

Rolling Rock

Hourglass Puzzle

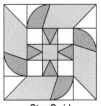

Star Swirl

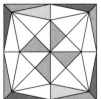

Secret Star

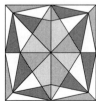

Diamond Star

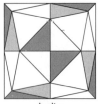

Jupiter

Uneven Star

Tumbling Star

 2 Contemporary Pieced
Spinning Suns

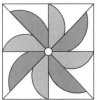

Black-Eyed Susan

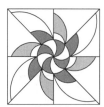

Sun Spin

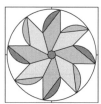

Star Dahlia

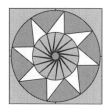

Kirsten's Star

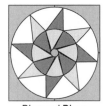

Diamond Diane

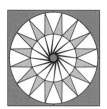

September Flower

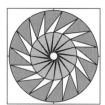

Nevada Star

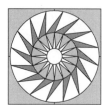

Rhode Island Star

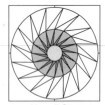

Hawaii Star

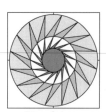

Dizzy Spinner

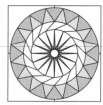

Blueberry Pie

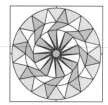

Rhubarb Pie

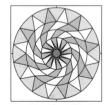

Key Lime Pie

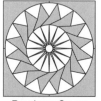

Raspberry Cream

Cool Mint Candy

Fireworks

2 Contemporary Pieced
Strip Quilts

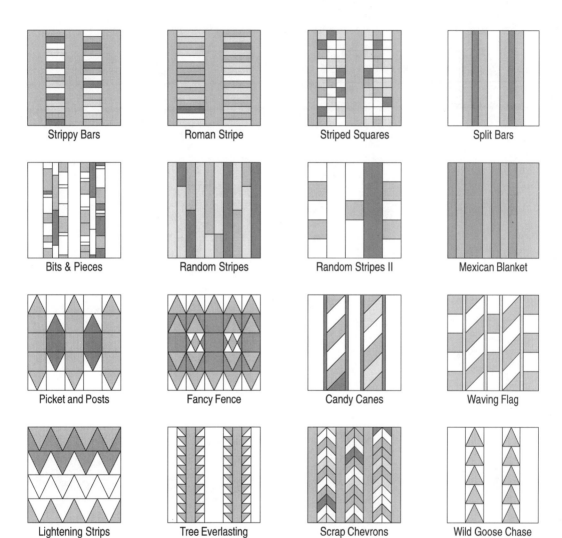

Strippy Bars	Roman Stripe	Striped Squares	Split Bars
Bits & Pieces	Random Stripes	Random Stripes II	Mexican Blanket
Picket and Posts	Fancy Fence	Candy Canes	Waving Flag
Lightening Strips	Tree Everlasting	Scrap Chevrons	Wild Goose Chase

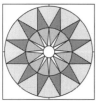

Sun Compass 1

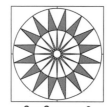

Sun Compass 2

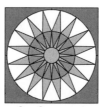

Sun Compass 3

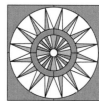

Sun Wheel 1

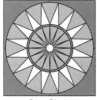

Sun Circle

Prairie Point Sun

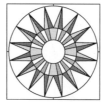

Sun Wheel 2

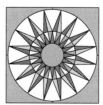

Star within Sun

South Pole Star

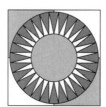

Dean's Sunflower
Sun

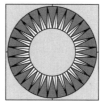

August Sun

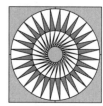

Sun Swirl

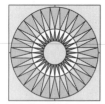

Sun Spokes

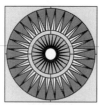

Sun Rings

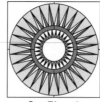

Sun Rings 2

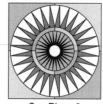

Sun Rings 3

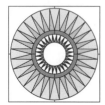

Sun Rings 4

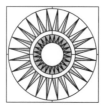

Sedona's Sun

Blue Shirt

Shirt & Sweater

Starched Shirt

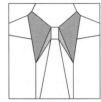

Work Shirt

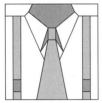

Suspenders

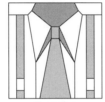

Executive

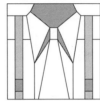

The Harvard Club

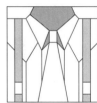

Country Lawyer

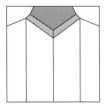

T-Shirt

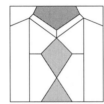

Logo T-Shirt

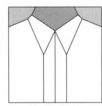

No Tie Shirt

Shirt and Sweater

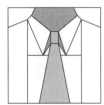

Stuffed Shirt

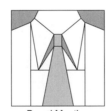

Bored Meeting

Pocket Protecter

Cowboy Shirt

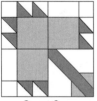

Sweet Gum

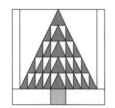

Snowy Pine

Sugar Maple

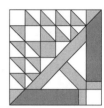

Hemlock

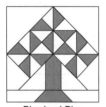

Pinwheel Pine

Christmas Pine

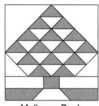

Mulberry Bush

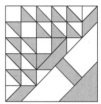

Blue Spruce

Birds in the Pine

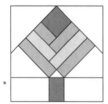

Log Cabin Tree

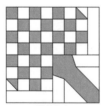

Old Oak

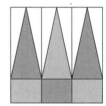

Topiary Trio

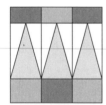

Topiary Trio Too

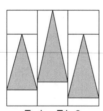

Topiary Trio 3

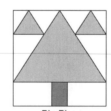

Big Pine

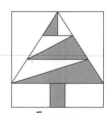

Evergreen

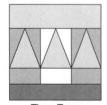

Three Trees

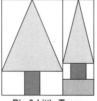

Big & Little Trees

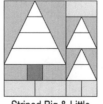

Striped Big & Little

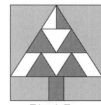

Triangle Tree

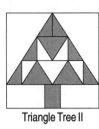

Triangle Tree II

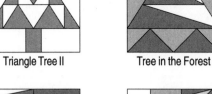

Tree in the Forest

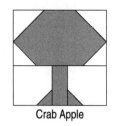

Crab Apple

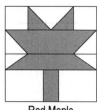

Red Maple

Diamond-in-the-Tree

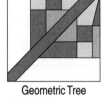

Geometric Tree

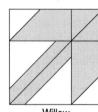

Willow

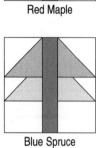

Blue Spruce

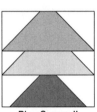

Blue Spruce II

Umbrella Tree

Tree on a Hill

3 Paper Piecing

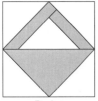

Basket

Striped Basket

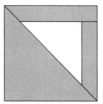

On-point Basket

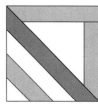

On-point Basket II

On-point Basket III

On-point Basket IV

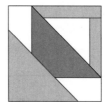

Basket on the Table

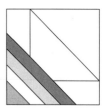

Bowl on Striped Cloth

Striped Bowl on Cloth

Basket

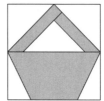

Big Basket

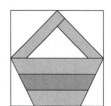

Big Striped Basket

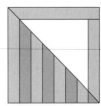

On-point Layered
Basket

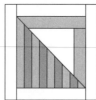

On-point Layered
Basket II

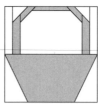

Curved-handle
Basket

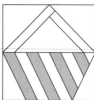

Layered Basket

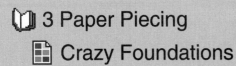

3 Paper Piecing
Crazy Foundations

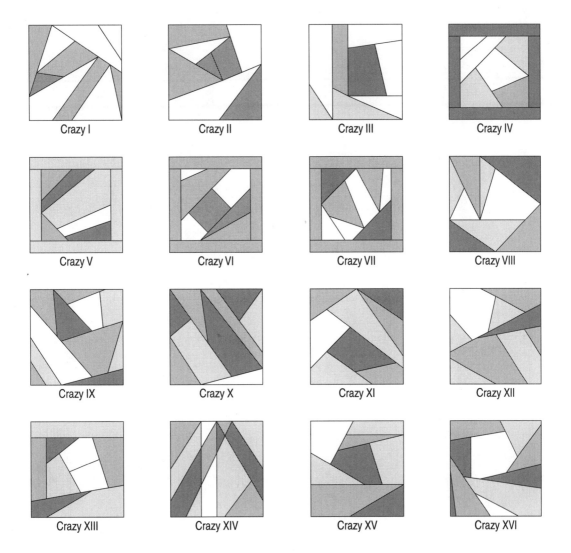

Crazy I	Crazy II	Crazy III	Crazy IV
Crazy V	Crazy VI	Crazy VII	Crazy VIII
Crazy IX	Crazy X	Crazy XI	Crazy XII
Crazy XIII	Crazy XIV	Crazy XV	Crazy XVI

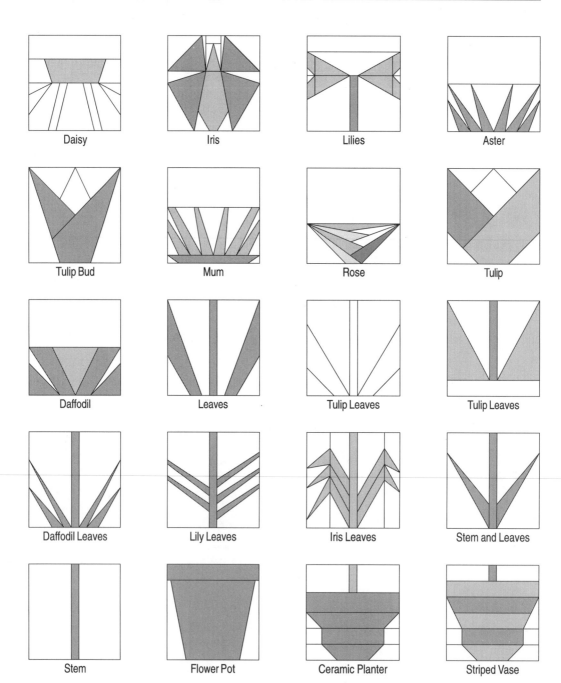

Daisy

Iris

Lilies

Aster

Tulip Bud

Mum

Rose

Tulip

Daffodil

Leaves

Tulip Leaves

Tulip Leaves

Daffodil Leaves

Lily Leaves

Iris Leaves

Stem and Leaves

Stem

Flower Pot

Ceramic Planter

Striped Vase

Crocus

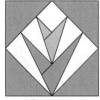

Snowdrop

Bluebell

Double Tulip

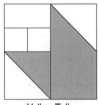

Yellow Tulip

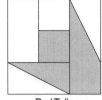

Red Tulip

Daffodil

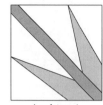

Leafstem 1

Leafstem 2

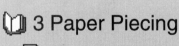

3 Paper Piecing
Flying Geese

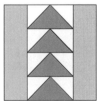

Flying Geese

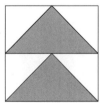

Flying Geese I

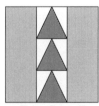

Flying Geese II

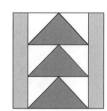

Flying Geese III

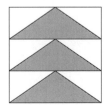

Flying Geese IV

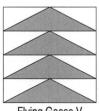

Flying Geese V

Flying Geese VI

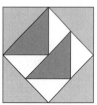

Flying Geese VII

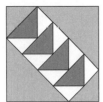

Flying Geese VIII

Flying Geese IX

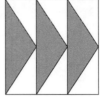

Flying Geese X

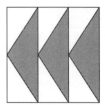

Flying Geese XI

Flying Geese XII

Flying Geese XIII

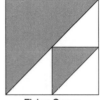

Flying Goose

Flying Goose
Variation

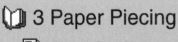

3 Paper Piecing
Fun Stuff

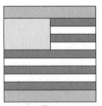

Flag

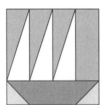

Schooner

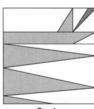

Snake

Sunrise

On-point Flag

On-point Flag II

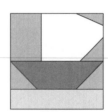

Sailboat

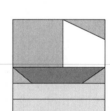

Sailboat II

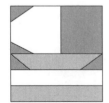

Sailboat III

Big Bird House

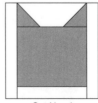

Cat Head

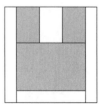

Rabbit Head

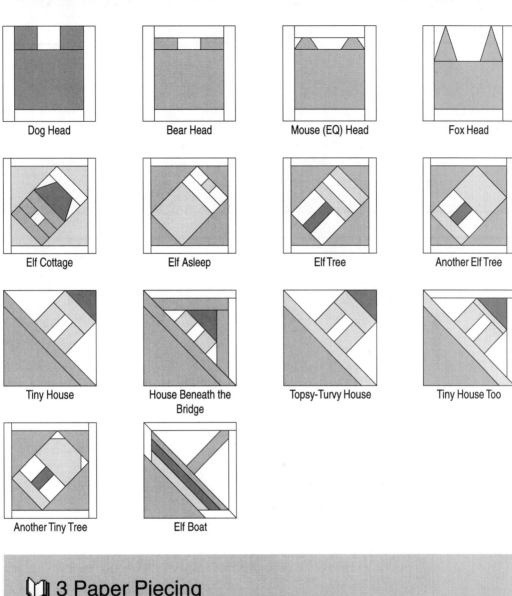

Dog Head

Bear Head

Mouse (EQ) Head

Fox Head

Elf Cottage

Elf Asleep

Elf Tree

Another Elf Tree

Tiny House

House Beneath the Bridge

Topsy-Turvy House

Tiny House Too

Another Tiny Tree

Elf Boat

3 Paper Piecing
Geometrics

Rail Fence

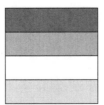

Rail Fence II

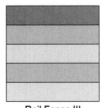

Rail Fence III

Diagonal Strips

Diagonal Strips II

Blocks in a Box

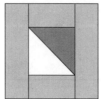

Blocks in a Box Variation

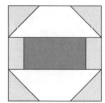

American Chain

Quarter Log Cabin

Cracker

Letter H

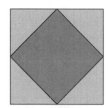

Diamond in the Square

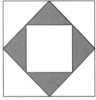

Economy Patch

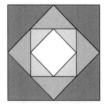

Twelve Triangles

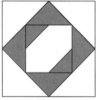

Album

Album II

Broken Band Variation

 3 Paper Piecing

 Hebrew Alphabet

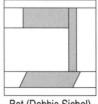

Aleph (Debbie Sichel)

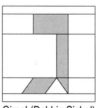

Bet (Debbie Sichel)

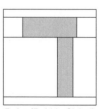

Gimel (Debbie Sichel)

Dalet (Debbie Sichel)

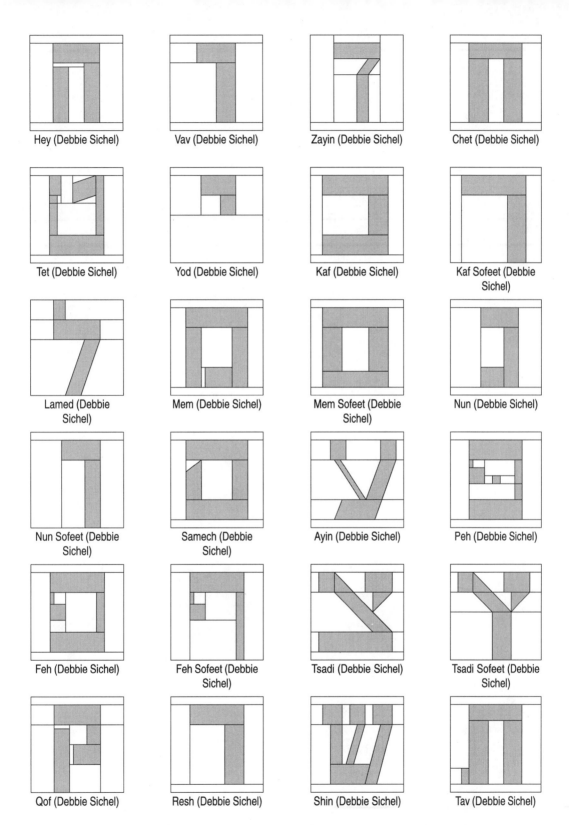

Hey (Debbie Sichel)

Vav (Debbie Sichel)

Zayin (Debbie Sichel)

Chet (Debbie Sichel)

Tet (Debbie Sichel)

Yod (Debbie Sichel)

Kaf (Debbie Sichel)

Kaf Sofeet (Debbie Sichel)

Lamed (Debbie Sichel)

Mem (Debbie Sichel)

Mem Sofeet (Debbie Sichel)

Nun (Debbie Sichel)

Nun Sofeet (Debbie Sichel)

Samech (Debbie Sichel)

Ayin (Debbie Sichel)

Peh (Debbie Sichel)

Feh (Debbie Sichel)

Feh Sofeet (Debbie Sichel)

Tsadi (Debbie Sichel)

Tsadi Sofeet (Debbie Sichel)

Qof (Debbie Sichel)

Resh (Debbie Sichel)

Shin (Debbie Sichel)

Tav (Debbie Sichel)

Pumpkin

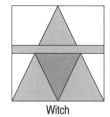

Witch

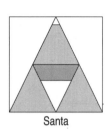

Santa

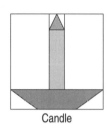

Candle

Pandora's Present

Surprise Package

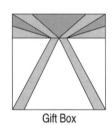

Gift Box

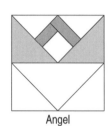

Angel

Fir Tree

Christmas Tree

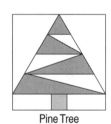

Pine Tree

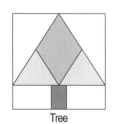

Tree

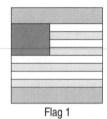

Flag 1

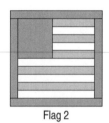

Flag 2

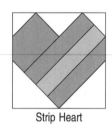

Strip Heart

Strip Heart II

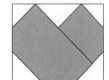

Heart

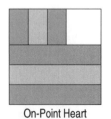

On-Point Heart

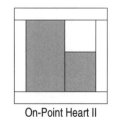

On-Point Heart II

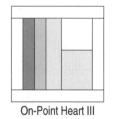

On-Point Heart III

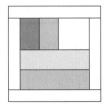
On-Point Heart IV

On-Point Heart V

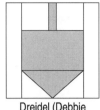
Dreidel (Debbie Sichel)

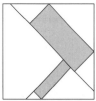
Grogger (Debbie Sichel)

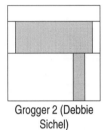
Grogger 2 (Debbie Sichel)

  3 Paper Piecing
In The Woods

Pine

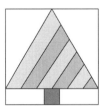
Fir

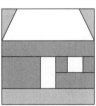
Little House

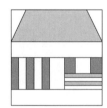
Log Cabin

Cabin

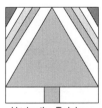
Under the Rainbow

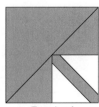
Easy Leaf

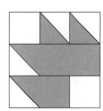
Maple Leaf

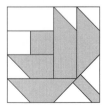
Maple Leaf

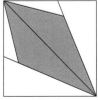
Leaf

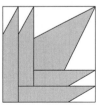
Silver Maple

Oak Leaf

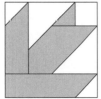
Red Oak

Sweetgum

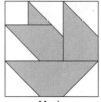
Maple

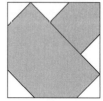
Ivy

3 Paper Piecing
Log Cabins

Off-Center Log Cabin

Wild Goose Log Cabin

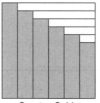
Quarter Cabin

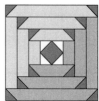
Diamond-in-Square Log Cabin

Diamond Center Log Cabin

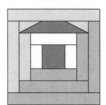
Log Cabin House

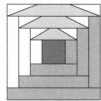
Log Cabin Pine

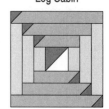
Marching Triangles

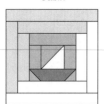
Log Cabin Boat

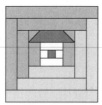
Wren House

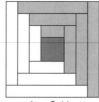
Log Cabin

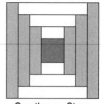
Courthouse Steps

Large Center Log Cabin

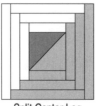
Split Center Log Cabin

Rectangle Center Log Cabin

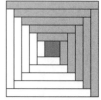
Log Cabin

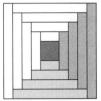

Log Cabin

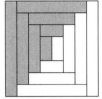

Log Cabin

Crazy Log Cabin

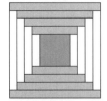

Courthouse Steps II

3 Paper Piecing
Pineapples

Pineapple

Pineapple II

Pineapple III

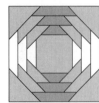

Pineapple IV

Pineapple V

Pineapple VI

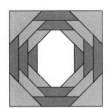

Pineapple VII

Pineapple VIII

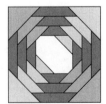

Pineapple IX

Pineapple X

Pineapple XI

Pineapple Album

Pineapple Album II

Pineapple Album III

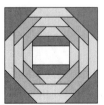

Pineapple Album IV

Pineapple Album V

Stained Glass
Diamond in Square

Stained Glass
Diamond in Square 2

Stained Glass
Diamond in Square 3

Stained Glass
Diamond in Square 4

Stained Glass
Diamond in Square 5

Stained Glass
Diamond with Borders

Stained Glass
Cracker

Stained Glass H

Stained Glass
Cracker 2

Stained Glass
Diamond in Square 6

Stained Glass 7 Twist

Stained Glass 6 Twist

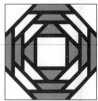

Stained Glass
Pineapple 1

Stained Glass
Pineapple 2

Stained Glass
Pineapple 3

Stained Glass
Pineapple 4

Stained Glass
Pineapple 5

Stained Glass Log
Cabin Triangle

Stained Glass Circle

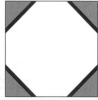

Stained Glass Blunt
Square on Point

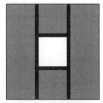

Stained Glass
Surrounded Square

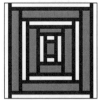

Stained Glass Log
Cabin Variation

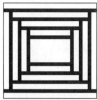

Stained Glass Log
Cabin Variation 2

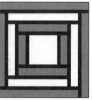

Stained Glass Log
Cabin

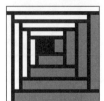

Stained Glass
Uneven Log Cabin

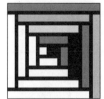

Stained Glass Log
Cabin 2

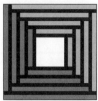

Stained Glass Log
Cabin 3

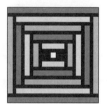

Stained Glass Log
Cabin 4

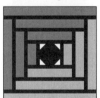

Stained Glass Log
Cabin 5

Stained Glass Log
Cabin 6

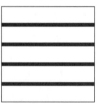

Stained Glass Stripes

Stained Glass
Stripes 2

3 Paper Piecing
Stained Glass Pictures

Stained Glass House

Stained Glass
House 2

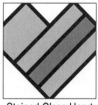

Stained Glass Heart

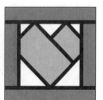

Stained Glass
Heart 2

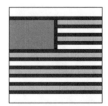

Stained Glass Flag

Stained Glass
Sailboat

Stained Glass Flower

Stained Glass Candle

Stained Glass Flower

Stained Glass Tree 1

Stained Glass Tree 2

Stained Glass Tree 3

Stained Glass
Pinetree 1

Stained Glass
Pinetree 2

Stained Glass
Pinetree 3

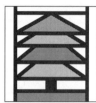

Stained Glass
Pinetree 4

 3 Paper Piecing

 Stained Glass Quarters

Quarter Woven Star

Quarter Woven Star 2

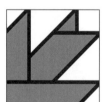

Quarter Crossing
Points

Quarter Star in a Star

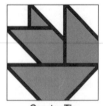

Quarter T's

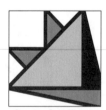

Quarter Star Flower

Quarter Star with
Triangles

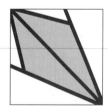

Quarter Leaf

Quarter Cross

Quarter Box-in-Box

Quarter Diagonal
Triangles

Quarter Windmill

Quarter Rose

Quarter Stripe with Diamond

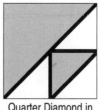

Quarter Diamond in Square

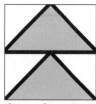

Quarter Geese Block

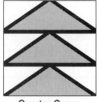

Quarter Geese Block 2

📖 3 Paper Piecing
🗒 Trees

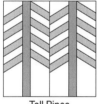

Tall Pines

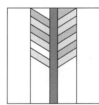

Tall Tree

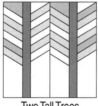

Two Tall Trees

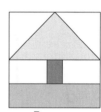

Evergreen

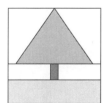

Evergreen I

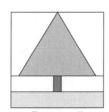

Evergreen II

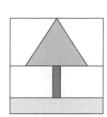

Evergreen III

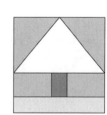

Evergreen IV

Evergreen & Shadow

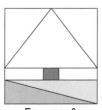

Evergreen & Shadow II

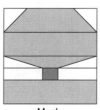

Maple

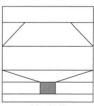

Maple II

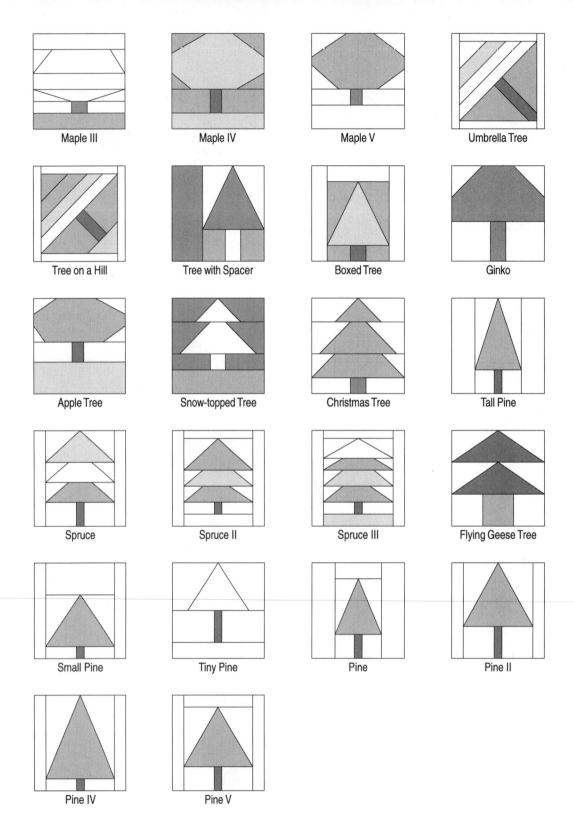

Maple III

Maple IV

Maple V

Umbrella Tree

Tree on a Hill

Tree with Spacer

Boxed Tree

Ginko

Apple Tree

Snow-topped Tree

Christmas Tree

Tall Pine

Spruce

Spruce II

Spruce III

Flying Geese Tree

Small Pine

Tiny Pine

Pine

Pine II

Pine IV

Pine V

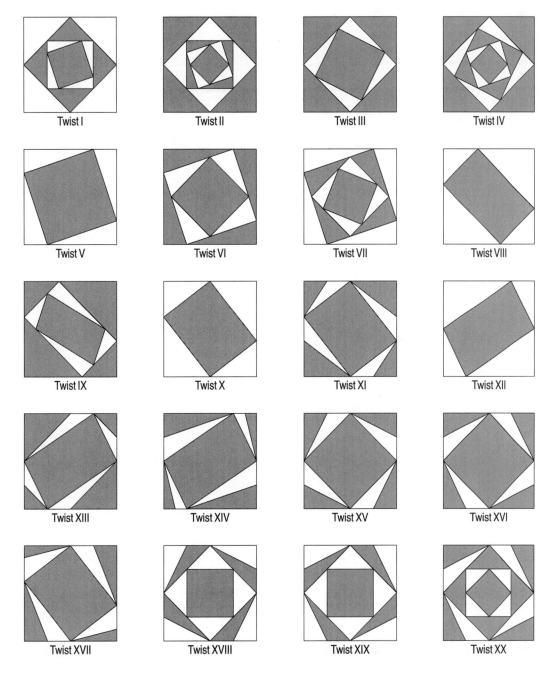

Twist I

Twist II

Twist III

Twist IV

Twist V

Twist VI

Twist VII

Twist VIII

Twist IX

Twist X

Twist XI

Twist XII

Twist XIII

Twist XIV

Twist XV

Twist XVI

Twist XVII

Twist XVIII

Twist XIX

Twist XX

Twist XXI

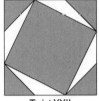

Twist XXII

Twist XXIII

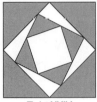

Twist XXIV

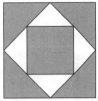

Economy Patch

4 Classic Appliqué

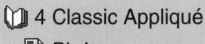

4 Classic Appliqué

Birds

Doves

Bird in Flight

Bird with Tail Feathers

Bird Standing

Tropical Bird

Bird Standing 2

Bird Standing 3

Folk Art Bird

Bluebird in Flight

Bluebird by Nancy
Cabot, 1944

Antique Dove

Antique Redbird

Bird from Album Quilt

Bird from Album
Quilt 2

Wren

Swan

Fancy Butterfly from
Grandmother Clark

Butterfly with Curling
Antennae

Butterfly with
Scalloped Wings

Butterflies in Flight

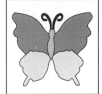

Butterfly from
Baltimore Album

Swallowtail Butterfly

Butterfly from 40s
Quilt

Butterfly from 30s
Quilt

Folk Art Butterfly

Butterfly from
Tennessee Quilt

Butterfly Ring

Butterfly Ring 2

Butterfly from 1936

Moth

Swallowtail Butterfly 2

Butterflies in Flight

Butterfly and Flower

Japanese Bamboo

Tulip Tree Leaves

Tulips

Oak Leaf and Acorn

Oak Leaves

Oak Leaf and
Acorn 2

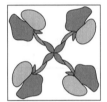

Sweet Peas

Tulips

Alabama Album Quilt

Mexican Rose

Mexican Rose 2

Mexican Rose 3

Crossing Roses

Bottle Brush

Bud Block

Peonies

English Rose

English Rose II

Lollipop Flowers

Mexican Rose

Circle Rose

Circle Rose II

Hearts & Sunflowers

Comb

Oak Leaf & Reel

Oak Leaf Wreath

Oak Leaf Wreath II

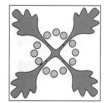

Oak Leaf Wreath III

Crossing Branches

19th-century Leaves

Baltimore Block

Trellis Vines

4 Classic Appliqué
Flowers

Tulip from North
Carolina Quilt

Tulip from North
Carolina Quilt 2

Tulip Applique

Poinsettia

Flower of Christmas
from Marie Webster

Single Flower

Flowers from Antique
Sampler Quilt

Flowers from Antique
Sampler Quilt 2

Poinsettia 2

Rose in Bud

Rose of Sharon from
Tennessee

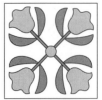

Tulip from North
Carolina

Black Tulip

Hearts and Flowers

Cock's Comb and
Currants

Bleeding Heart from
Grandma Dexter

 4 Classic Appliqué

 Flowers in Vases

Basket Variation

Vase with Mixed
Bouquet

Tulips from 1855
Album Quilt

Flowers in Pitcher

Tiger Lily

Tulip Bowl from North
Carolina

English Flower Pot

Nosegay Quilt from
McKim Studios

Tulips in Pot

Bouquet from Album
Quilt

Flowers in Heart Vase

Horn of Plenty

Kentucky Flowerpot

Rose of Sharon

Kansas Beauty

Tulips in Urn

4 Classic Appliqué
Flowers On-Point

Flowers from Antique Sampler

Flower Pot

Kansas Beauty On-Point

Tulips in Urn On-Point

Rose of Sharon On-Point

Nebraska Tulips

North Carolina Tulip

Lily Pond from Ladies Art Company

Tulip Applique

Tulip Garden

Dutch Tulip

Tulip and Sun

First-place Flower

Rose & Buds

Three-Part Flower

Three-Part Flower II

Stencil Tulips

Tulip Tree

Large Tulip

Posey

Pennsylvania Dutch

Folk Tulip

Mexican Rose

Rose

📖 4 Classic Appliqué
🗐 Folk Art Blocks

Rooster Weathervane

Eagle with Berries

Folk Bird

Pennsylvania Dutch

Wreath Stencil

Hex Sign

Old German Design

American Star

Pineapple ca. 1850

Pineapple Design

Coxcomb in Pot

Folk Art Flower

Pennsylvania Tulip

Pomegranate

Antique Baltimore
Album House

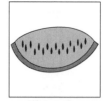

Watermelon

4 Classic Appliqué
Grape and Vine Borders

Relaxed Corner (In)

Relaxed Corner (Out)

Relaxed Corner (Out)
with Grapes

Relaxed Vine

Relaxed Vine with
Grapes

Relaxed Vine with
Grapes and Leaves

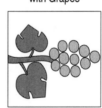

Relaxed Grape Vine

Tight Corner (In)

Tight Corner (Out)

Tight Corner (Out)
with Grapes

Tight Vine

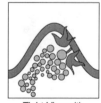

Tight Vine with
Grapes

Tight Vine with
Grapes and Leaves

Tight Grape Vine

Grapes

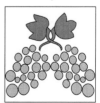

Double Grapes

Grapes On-point

4 Classic Appliqué

Roses

Rose in Bloom

Rose of Sharon

Rose of LeMoyne

Rose Applique

Rose of Sharon

Rose Bouquet with Stars

Rose Tree

Rose of Sharon from McKim Studios

Rose of Sharon

Old Rose of Sharon from Canada

Radical Rose

Old Tulips

Rose from New Jersey Sampler

Topeka Rose

Rose of Sharon

Rosebuds

Rose Wreath II

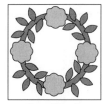

Rose Wreath

Rose Ring

Cabbage Rose
Wreath

Rose of Sharon
Wreath

📖 4 Classic Appliqué
🔲 Silhouettes

Cow

Deer

Dog

Bowl of Fruit

Hen and Chicks

Horse

Man

Woman

Rooster

Kissing Birds

Birds on Bough

Eagle with Talons

Eagle

Eagle

Butterfly

Simple Bird

 4 Classic Appliqué

 Sunbonnet Sue

Sunbonnet Girl with
Watering Can

Sunbonnet Girl with
Bouquet

Colonial Lady

Dutch Girl

Bonnet Baby Girl
from McKim Studios

Bonnet Baby Boy
from McKim Studios

Sunbonnet Sue

Valentine Sue

Bashful Sam

Sunbonnet Sue

Sunny Jim

Sue Picks Tulips

Overall Bill

Sue Redux

Sam

Sue with Balloons

Sue On-point

4 Classic Appliqué
Wreaths

Rose and Tulip from
Grandma Dexter

Rose Wreath from
New Jersey Sampler

Floral Wreath from
Grandma Dexter

Christmas Cactus

Cherry Wreath

Oak and Acorn
Wreath

Valentine Wreath

Hearts & Ribbons

Forget-Me-Not Ring

Ribbon Medallion

Nosegay Wreath

Forget-Me-Not
Wreath

Wildflower Wreath

Wildflower Ring

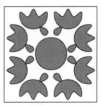

Tulip Ring

Flower Wreath

Flower Wreath II

Reel

5 Contemporary Appliqué

5 Contemporary Appliqué
Bugs

Bee

Bumble Bee

Housefly

Wasp

Lacewing

Grasshopper

Praying Mantis

Beetle

Beetle

Beetle

Beetle

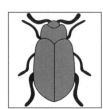
Beetle

Beetle

Ladybug

Beetle

VW Beetle

5 Contemporary Appliqué

Cats

Abyssinian Cat

Tabby

Burmese Cat

Maine Coon Cat

Snowshoe Cat

Oriental Short Hair

Sleepy Cat

Cat

Calico Cartoon Cat

Smiling Cartoon Cat

Prowling Cat
Silhouette

Standing Cat
Silhouette

Sitting Cat Silhouette

Hungry Cat
Silhouette

Walking Cat
Silhouette

Cartoon Cat
Silhouette

5 Contemporary Appliqué

Celebrations

Mates for Life (Rita Denenberg)

Our Wedding (Rita Denenberg)

Peonies and Lilacs (Rita Denenberg)

Our Vase (Rita Denenberg)

Ribbon

Dove Corner Block (Rita Denenberg)

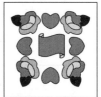

Information Please (Rita Deneberg)

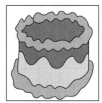

Cake

Gift Package

Gift Package

Gift Package

Family Tree (Rita Denenberg)

Our House (Rita Denenberg)

Stork and Baby

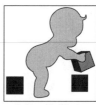

Baby with Blocks

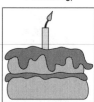

Baby's First Birthday

5 Contemporary Appliqué
Children

Girl with Toy Cat

Baby Bath

Little Bo Peep and Sheep

Humpty Dumpty

Bird and Bell Toy

Boy and Butterfly

Boy and Dog

Puppy

Boy with Cake

Giraffe Toy

Giraffe Toy

Ballerina

Birthday Toys and Ribbon

Girl with Chicks

Boy with Train

Elephant Toy

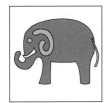
Elephant Toy

Bunny with Tulip (Rita Denenberg)

Teddy Bear with Tulip (Rita Denenberg)

5 Contemporary Appliqué
Christmas

Sleigh

Reindeer

Stocking

Santa

Angel with Harp

Teddy Bear and Gift

Rocking Horse

Drum

Gift

Horn

Bell

Snowman

Bells with Holly

Ornaments with Holly

Dove Ornament

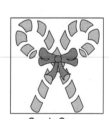
Candy Canes

Holly

Ornament with Star

Ribbon

Holly Border

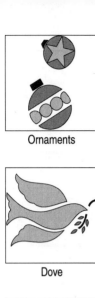

Ornaments

Star

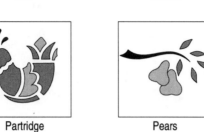

Candle

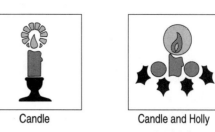

Candle and Holly

Dove

Partridge

Pears

Poinsettia

Snowflake

Wreath

Nutcracker

Angel with Candle

Rudolph the Red-Nosed Reindeer

Poinsettia

Ann's Angel

Candle and Holder

Christmas Tree

Tree in the Snow

Candle

Peace Dove (Rita Denenberg)

Angel (Rita Denenberg)

Christmas Tree (Rita Denenberg)

Wise Men (Rita Denenberg)

Presents (Rita Denenberg)

Christ Child (Rita Denenberg)

Christmas Stocking (Rita Denenberg)

Fireplace at Christmas (Rita Denenberg)

Pointsettia Border (Rita Denenberg)

Ring Those Bells (Rita Denenberg)

Noel (Rita Denenberg)

Wreath (Rita Denenberg)

Coming Home (Rita Denenberg)

Polar Bear

Polar Bear and Stars

Penguin

📖 5 Contemporary Appliqué
🗓 Day in the Country

Christmas Goose

Christmas Goose

Goose

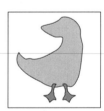

Goose

Duck

Duck II

Duckling

Hen

Rooster

Hen

Pig

Pig

Cow

Horse

Bluebird on Branch

Robin on Branch

Birdhouse

Flying Home

Birdhouse

Nest with Eggs

Tree of Life

Bird on a Fence

Cardinal

Bird

Bird II

Bird III

Heart

Biker (Rita Denenberg)

Sunbonnet (Rita Denenberg)

Dress on a Clothes-line

Dotted Dress

Dress with Buttons

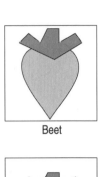

Beet

Carrot

Turnip

Eggplant

Tomato

Radish

Seed Packet Row
Marker

Seed Packet Row
Marker II

Strawberry

Apple

Pea Pods on Vine

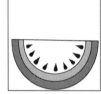

Watermelon Slice

Curly Flower with
Center

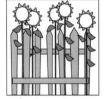

Sunflower Fence

Watering Can

Ann's Garden Wreath

Butterfly

Butterfly II

Butterfly III

Butterfly IV

Butterflies

Butterflies and
Blossom

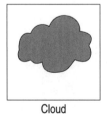

Cloud

Two Clouds

Thundercloud

Sun

Man in the Moon

Crescent Moon

Big Dipper

Little Dipper

📖 5 Contemporary Appliqué
🗒 Easter

Rabbit

Rabbit

Easter Rabbit 1 (Rita Denenberg)

Easter Rabbit 2 (Rita Denenberg)

Easter Rabbit 3 (Rita Denenberg)

Bunny

Sheep

Chick (Rita Denenberg)

Duckling in Shell

Squirrel

Easter Egg (Rita Denenberg)

Easter Egg 2 (Rita Denenberg)

Bunny with Egg (Rita Denenberg)

Easter Egg

Easter Lily (Rita Deneberg)

Easter Basket (Rita Denenberg)

 5 Contemporary Appliqué

 Fish

Goldie Fish

Edward Scissortail Fish

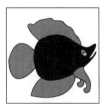

Rudy Fish

Skipper Fish

Chloe Fish

Bud Fish

Flash Fish

Tiger Fish

Bubbles Fish

Carpie Fish

Angel Fish

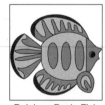

Rainbow Rosie Fish

Smoochie Fish

Jelly Bean Fish

Rocky Fish

Zoe Fish

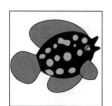

Scaley Fish

Zorro Fish

Fins Fish

Gilbert Fish

Spike Fish

Sharky Fish

Guppy Fish

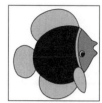

Wally Fish

Starfish

📖 5 Contemporary Appliqué
▦ Flowers

Flower Sprig

Tulips

Black-Eyed Susans

Bouquet

Flowers

Tulips

Flower and Leaves

Tulip

Carnation (Rita Denenberg)

Lily (Rita Denenberg)

Pansy (Rita Denenberg)

Tiger Lily (Rita Denenberg)

Lily of the Valley (Rita Denenberg)

Gardenia (Rita Denenberg)

Sunflower (Rita Denenberg)

Rose (Rita Denenberg)

Peony (Rita Denenberg)

Lilacs (Rita Denenberg)

Daffodil (Rita Denenberg)

Bleeding Heart (Rita Denenberg)

Iris - vertical (Rita Denenberg)

Iris - on point (Rita Denenberg)

Heart of My Hearts (Rita Denenberg)

We Grew Roses (Rita Denenberg)

Rose Border (Rita Denenberg)

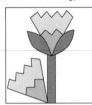

Two Buds

Two Buds 2

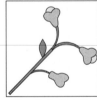

Blue Buds (quarter design)

Summer Block (quarter design)

Dahlia

Rose

Anemones (quarter design)

Flower in the Grass

Daisy

Peony

Three-Part Flower

Three-Part Flower II

Rose and Buds

Rosebud

Stencil Tulips

Tulip Block

Tulip Block II

Large Tulip

Tulip Tree

Wreath (Rita Denenberg)

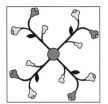

Blue Buds

Summer Block

Poppies

Tyrolean Design

Shamrocks

Bouquet

Flower Pot

Flower Pot II

Wildflower Bouquet

Sunflowers in a Pot

Painted Pot

Roses and Butterfly

Bird in the Buds

Garden Gate (Rita Denenberg)

Antique Birdcage (Rita Denenberg)

 5 Contemporary Appliqué

Hearts

Stars and Hearts Forever

Heart with Candybox Ruffle

Heart of Leaves

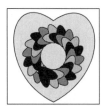

Heart Ring

Garden of Hearts

Celtic Hearts with Leaves

Celtic Hearts

Heart Flower Bouquet

Single Celtic Heart

Gumdrop Heart

Four Hearts

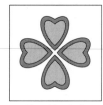

Four Hearts II

Four Hearts III

Double Hearts

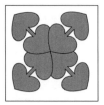

Heart Blossoms

Broken Heart

Heart Flower

Heart Flower II

Corner Hearts

Eight Hearts

Crossing Hearts

Split Heart

My Hearts of Hearts
(Rita Denenberg)

5 Contemporary Appliqué
Holiday

Shamrocks

Hat and Pipe

Cupid

Hanukkah (Rita
Denenberg)

David Star (Rita
Denenberg)

Dreidel (Rita
Denenberg)

Kikombe cha Umoja
(Unity Cup)

Bendera (Kwanzaa
Flag)

Mishumaa (7 Candles) &
Kinara (Candle Holder)

Muhindi (Corn)

Mazao (The Crops)

Trick or Treat Pumpkin

Pumpkin

Witch (Rita Denenberg)

Black Cat (Rita Denenberg)

Trick RTreat (Rita Denenberg)

Jack O'Lantern (Rita Denenberg)

Ghost (Rita Denenberg)

Bats in Web (Rita Denenberg)

 5 Contemporary Appliqué

 Music

Sax (Rita Denenberg)

Saxophone

Saxophone with Notes

Violin (Rita Denenberg)

Big Bass (Rita Denenberg)

Guitar

Violin

Trumpet

Clarinet (Rita Denenberg)

"88" (Rita Denenberg)

Piano

Drum (Rita Denenberg)

Drum and Sticks

Musical Signs (Rita Denenberg)

Treble Clef

Treble Staff

Bass Clef

Bass Staff

Musical Note I

Musical Note II

Musical Note III

The Maestro (Rita Denenberg)

 5 Contemporary Appliqué

 Sports

Football

Football (Rita Denenberg)

Football Helmet (Rita Denenberg)

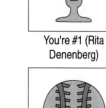

You're #1 (Rita Denenberg)

Basketball Hoop (Rita Denenberg)

Basketball

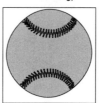

Baseball

Baseball (Rita Denenberg)

Soccer ball

Bowling Ball (Rita Denenberg)

Bowling Pin (Rita Denenberg)

Golfball (Rita Denenberg)

The 18th Hole (Rita Denenberg)

Ice Skates (Rita Denenberg)

Roller Blade (Rita Denenberg)

Gone Fishin' (Rita Denenberg)

Boxing Gloves (Rita Denenberg)

Baseball Cap (Rita Denenberg)

 5 Contemporary Appliqué

Teddy Bears

Teddy Bear 1

Teddy Bear 2

Teddy Bear 3

Teddy Bear 4

Teddy Bear 5

Teddy Bear 6

Teddy Bear 7

Teddy Bear 8

Teddy Bear with Ball

Teddy Bear with Honey

Teddy Bear with Shirt

Teddy Bear with Vest

Teddy Bear with Ice Cream

Teddy Bear with Block

Teddy Bear with Daisy

Teddy Bear with Daisy 2

Teddy Bear with Daisy 3

Teddy Bear with Flowers

 5 Contemporary Appliqué

 Tile and Celtic Designs

Arabesque

Moorish Tile

Fleur de Lis

Arabia

Alhambra Tile

Peacock Feathers

Byzantium

Mosaic

Islamic Tile

Grecian Tile

Roman Villa

Pompeii

Celtic Patch

Celtic Patch 2

Celtic Patch 3

Celtic Patch 4

Celtic Patch 5

Celtic Patch 6

Celtic Patch 7

Puzzle Patch

Interlocking Squares

Interlocking Squares
(border)

Ring Chain (corner)

Interlocking Rings
(border)

Interlocking Rings

5 Contemporary Appliqué

 Toys

Brontosaurus

Stegosaurus

Parasauroplophus

Triceratops

Deinonychus

Tricycle

Bike

Car

Hot Air Balloon

Toy Duck

Carousel Horse (Rita Denenberg)

China Doll (Rita Denenberg)

Jack-in-the-Box

Clown Doll

Duck Pull-toy

Ted E. Bear

Train Engine Wind-up

Tractor

Car

Plane (Rita Denenberg)

Plane

Sailboat

Sailboat II

Sailboat III

Rocket

Toy Rocket

World Globe

Spaceman Doll

Rocket

Robot I

Robot II

 5 Contemporary Appliqué

Your Design Studio

Needle & Thread
(Rita Denenberg)

Spool of Thread (Rita
Denenberg)

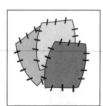

Patches (Rita
Denenberg)

Scissors (Rita
Denenberg)

Pincushion (Rita
Denenberg)

Rotary Cutter (Rita
Denenberg)

Thimble (Rita
Denenberg)

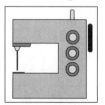

Sewing Machine

Bolt of Fabric

Spool of Thread

Computer Monitor

Keyboard

Telephone

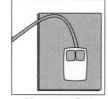

Mouse and Pad

Magnifying Glass

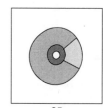

CD

Floppy

Non-pc Computer

Computer Tower

Me (Rita Denenberg)

6 Motifs

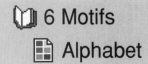
A

a

B

b

C

c

D

d

E

e

F

f

G

g

H

h

I

i

J

j

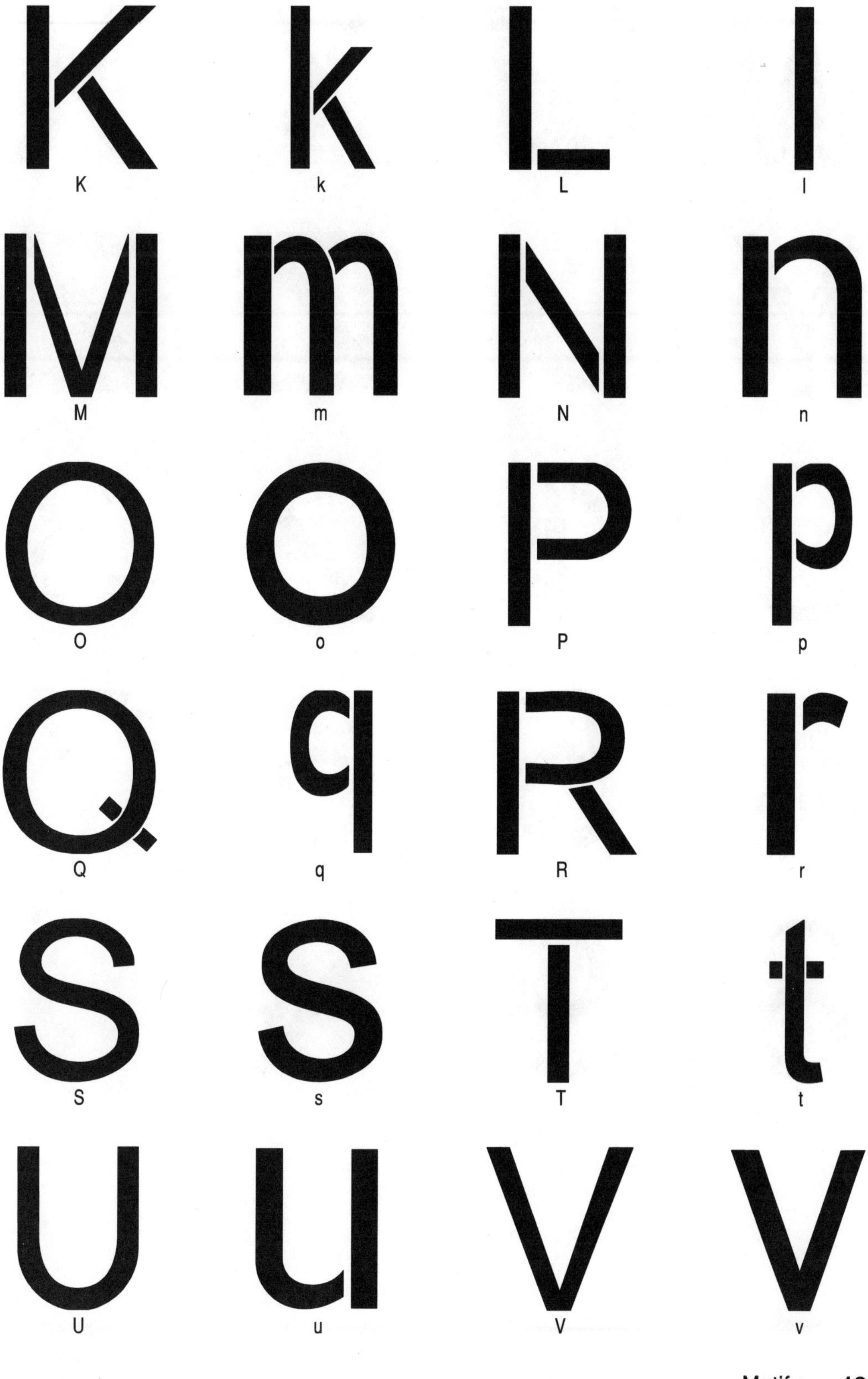

K k L l

M m N n

O o P p

Q q R r

S s T t

U u V v

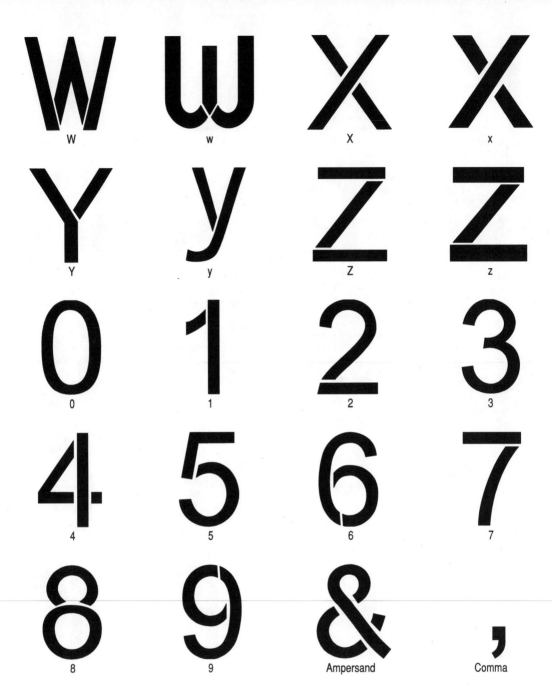

W

w

X

x

Y

y

Z

z

0

1

2

3

4

5

6

7

8

9

Ampersand

Comma

Period

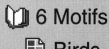

Antique Bird

Antique Dove

Eagle

Folk Art Bird

Wren

Bluebird in Flight

Standing Bird 2

Standing Bird 3

Bluebird by Nancy
Cabot, 1944

Bird from Album Quilt

Bird from Album
Quilt 2

Bird on House

Tropical Bird

Swan

Bird in Flight

Rooster

Bluebird on Branch

Robin on Branch

Cardinal

Flying Bird

Bird

Bird II

Duck

Duck II

Duckling

Goose

Bird in the Buds

Birdhouse

 6 Motifs

 Butterflies

Butterfly

Folk Art Butterfly

Butterfly from
30s Quilt

Swallowtail Butterfly

Butterfly from
Baltimore Album

Butterfly

Butterfly II

Butterfly III

Butterfly IV

Butterflies

Butterflies and
Blossom

Butterfly with
Scalloped Wings

Swallowtail Butterfly 2

Moth

Butterfly from 1936

Butterflies in Flight

 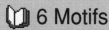

6 Motifs
Fish & Water Lilies

Goldie Fish

Edward Scissortail Fish

Rudy Fish

Skipper Fish

Chloe Fish

Bud Fish

Flash Fish

Tiger Fish

Bubbles Fish

Carpie Fish

Angel Fish

Rainbow Rosie Fish

Smoochie Fish

Jelly Bean Fish

Rocky Fish

Zoe Fish

Scaley Fish

Zorro Fish

Fins Fish

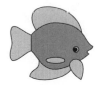

Gilbert Fish

Spike Fish

Sharky Fish

Guppy Fish

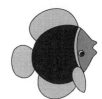

Wally Fish

Water Lily Pad

Water Lily

Water Lily II

Water Lily Pads

Water Lily Pads II

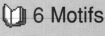

Reeds

6 Motifs
Flower Heads

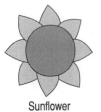

Sunflower

Double Tulip

Tulip and Leaves

Tulip Heads

Rose of Sharon

Zinnia

Pansy

Bud and Berries

Daffodil

Blossoms

Jonquil

Peony

Daisy

Violet Nosegay

Carnation

Orchid

 6 Motifs

 Flowers with Stems

North Carolina Tulip

Old Rose of Sharon
from Canada

Rose Bouquet

Single Flower

Black-Eyed Susan

Rose with Bud

Rose and Buds

Rose of LeMoyne

Rose Tree

Folk Art Flower

Flower from the 30s

Blossom and Berries

Lily

Scilla

Flower of Christmas
from Marie Webster

Rose Bud

Rose Applique

Pennysylvania Dutch
Flower

Daisy

Posey

Small Tulip

Pennsylvania Dutch

Rose

Circle Rose

Gloxinia

Folk Tulip

Mexican Rose

Coneflower

Coneflower II

Black-Eyed Susan

English Rose

Sunflower in Heart

Fantasy Flower

Old-Fashioned Tulip

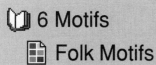

6 Motifs
Folk Motifs

Folk Art Leaf Motif

Pineapple Design

Folk Bird

Old German Design

Folk Art Flower

Hex Sign

Pomegranate

Folk Bird

Rooster Weathervane

Coxcomb in Pot

Pennsylvania Dutch

Pennsylvania Tulip

Eagle with Berries

Watermelon

American Star

Wreath Stencil

Eagle

6 Motifs
Fruits and Veggies

Apple

Pear

Orange

Grapes

Cherries

Strawberry

Watermelon Slice

Beet

Carrot

Turnip

Eggplant

Tomato

Radish

Pea Pod

Peas in Pods

Corn on the Cob

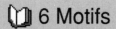 # 6 Motifs

 ## Landscape Elements

Snow-covered Tree	Man in the Moon	Little Dipper	Cloud
Big Dipper	Two Clouds	Twinkling Stars	Three Clouds
Star Group	Moon	Snow-covered Cabin	Smoke
Star	Moon N Stars	Moonlight	Moonlight II

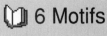 6 Motifs

 Leaves

Sweet Gum

Silver Maple

Shagbark Hickory

Stencil Leaf

White Oak

Grape Leaves

Elm

Box Elder

Palmate Leaf

Tree of Heaven

Grape Leaf

Honey Locust

Elm II

Grape Leaf II

Folk Art Leaf

Folk Art Leaf II

Antique Applique
Leaves

Baltimore Album Leaf

Holly

Folk Oak

Sassafras

Antique Applique Oak

Antique Applique Maple

Antique Applique Oak

Maple Leaf

Dozen-leaf Stem

Dozen-leaf Stem II

Dozen-leaf Stem III

Eleven-leaf Stem

Sycamore Leaf

Leaf Sprig

Laurel Leaves

13-leaf Stem

Oak Leaf

 6 Motifs

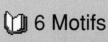 **Silhouettes**

Cat Silhouette

Cow Silhouette

Deer Silhouette

Dog Silhouette

Fruit Bowl Silhouette

Hen with Chicks
Silhouette

Horse Silhouette

Man Silhouette

Woman Silhouette

Rooster Silhouette

Kissing Birds
Silhouette

Birds on Branch
Silhouette

Eagle Silhouette

Eagle Silhouette II

Sitting Cat Silhouette

Hungry Cat
Silhouette

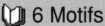

 6 Motifs

Simple Designs

Sun

Heart

Star

Moon

Ice Cream Cone

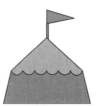
Tent

Balloons

Rainbow

Flower

Cow

Moorish Design

Happy Face

House

Tree

Apple Tree

Leaf

6 Motifs
Sports

Football

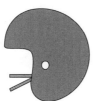

Football Helmet

Basketball

Basketball Hoop (Rita Denenberg)

Baseball

Baseball Cap (Rita Denenberg)

Volleyball

Ice Skate (Rita Denenberg)

Roller Skate (Rita Denenberg)

Bowling Ball (Rita Denenberg)

Bowling Pin (Rita Denenberg)

You're #1 (Rita Denenberg)

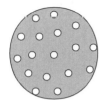

Golf Ball (Rita
Denenberg)

The 18th Hole (Rita
Denenberg)

Ball

Boxing Gloves (Rita
Denenberg)

Gone Fishin' (Rita
Denenberg)

6 Motifs

Sunbonnet Motifs

Sunbonnet Sue

Sitting Sue

Sue with Pocket

Sue Redux

Sun Bonnet Girl from
Grandmother Clark, 1931

Sun Bonnet Girl from
Grandmother Clark, 1931

Colonial Girl

Sunbonnet Sue as
Little Bo Peep

Sunbonnet Sue as
Little Boy Blue

Valentine Sue

Sue Picks Tulips

Sue with Balloons

Sam

Bashful Sam

Sunny Jim

Overall Bill

📖 6 Motifs
🔲 Wreaths

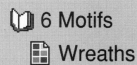

Cosmos Wreath

Wind Blown Rose

Scattered Roses

Tulips in a Tangle

Rose and Buds
Quatrefoil

Daisy Cluster

Rose Sprigs

Tulip Ring

Zinnia Ring

Scattered Blossoms

Buds in a Circle

Grape Leaf Wreath

Stencil Leaf Wreath

Oak Leaf Wreath

Antique Leaf Wreath

Hickory Wreath

7 Quilting Stencils

Continuous Line
Stars

Continuous Line Fish

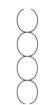

Continuous Line
Ovals

Continuous Line
Double Ovals

Fall Meander

Ribbon Meander

Continuous Line
Houses

Feather Meander

Continuous Line
Summer

Continuous Line
Winter

Continuous Line
Spring

Continuous Line Fall

Continuous Line
Feathers

Continuous Line
Flowers

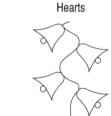

Continuous Line
Hearts

Heart & Ribbon
Meander

Leaf Meander

Continuous Line
Moon & Stars

Continuous Line Bells

Continuous Line
Maple Leaves

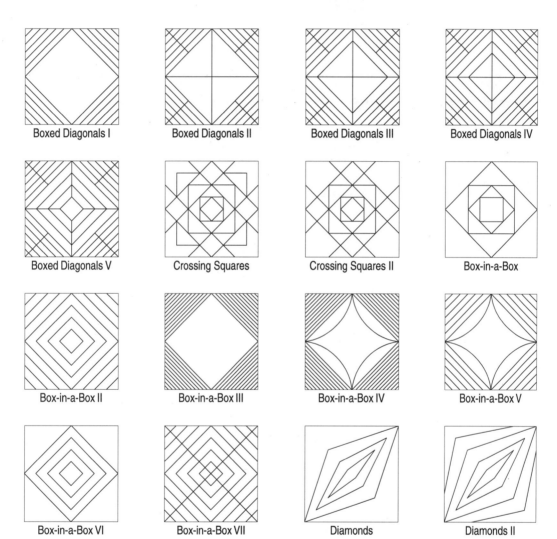

Boxed Diagonals I	Boxed Diagonals II	Boxed Diagonals III	Boxed Diagonals IV
Boxed Diagonals V	Crossing Squares	Crossing Squares II	Box-in-a-Box
Box-in-a-Box II	Box-in-a-Box III	Box-in-a-Box IV	Box-in-a-Box V
Box-in-a-Box VI	Box-in-a-Box VII	Diamonds	Diamonds II

Celtic Circle

Interlocking Rings

Rings and Squares

Celtic Interweave

Celtic Squares and Loops

Celtic Rope

Rings and Squares 2

Celtic Squares and Loops 2

Interwoven Square

Looped Rings

Interlocking Squares

Celtic Squares and Loops 3

Ring Chain (corner)

Interlocking Rings (border)

Interlocking Rings

Interlocking Squares (border)

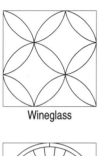
Wineglass

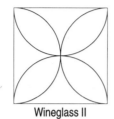
Wineglass II

Interlocking Lines

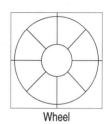
Wheel

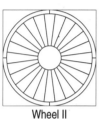
Wheel II

Circle-in-a-Circle

Circle-in-a-Circle II

Off-side Circles

Four Off-Side Circles

Pumpkin Seeds

Pumpkin Seeds II

Pumpkin Seeds III

Clover

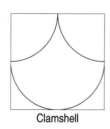
Clamshell

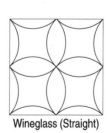
Wineglass (Straight)

Seeds & Waves

7 Quilting Stencils

Feathers

Feather (vertical)

Feather

Feather Plume with Ovals

Feathers with Heart

Feathers 4

Feathers 5

Feathers 6

Twisting Feathers

Twisting Feathers 2

Feather Ring

Crossing Feathers

Feathers with Heart Mirrored

Feather (corner)

Feather (border)

Double Plume

Double-Plume Medallion

7 Quilting Stencils
Hearts

Staggered Hearts

Dozen Hearts

Nine Hearts

Double-Heart Ring

Heart Ring

Heart Ring 2

Heart Stars

Six Star Ring

Six Heart Ring 2

Heart Tulip Ring

Rolling Hearts

Rolling Hearts 2

Rolling Hearts 3

Rolling Hearts 4

Rose Window

Double-Crossed Hearts

📖 7 Quilting Stencils
🗋 Hearts, Ribbons, Leaves

Crossing Ribbons

Rose Wreath

Tulip Ring

Ring of Hearts

Blossoms

Ribbons and Hearts

Heart Ring

Oak Leaves and Circles

Oak Leaves and Reel

Oak Leaves and Nuts

Radiating Petals

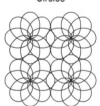

Four Radiating Petals

Swirling Petals

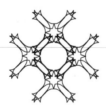

Ribbons and Stars

Oak Leaf and Hearts Reel

Ribbons and Hearts 2

Maple Leaves

Maple Leaf Ring

Leaves

Leaf Wreath with 4 Points

Small Leaf Wreath with 4 Points

Leaf Wreath with 5 Points

Leaf Wreath with 6 Points

Leaf Wreath

Leaves and Hearts

Oak Leaf and Reel

Oak Leaves and Berries

Leaves

Leaves II

Leaf Cable

Leaf Ring

Leaf Ring 2

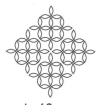

Leaf Square

7 Quilting Stencils
Stars and Snowflakes

Crystal Snowflake

Christmas Snowflake

Snowflake

Snowflake II

Snowflake III

Snowflake IV

Stars & Beams

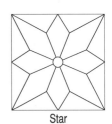

Star

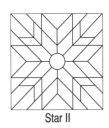

Star II

Star-in-Square

Starburst

Stars

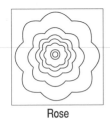

Rose

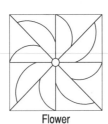

Flower

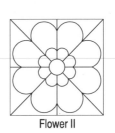

Flower II

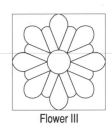

Flower III

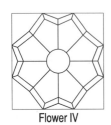

Flower IV

Tile Floor

Arabesque

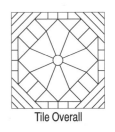

Tile Overall

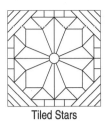

Tiled Stars

7 Quilting Stencils
Straight and Curved Lines

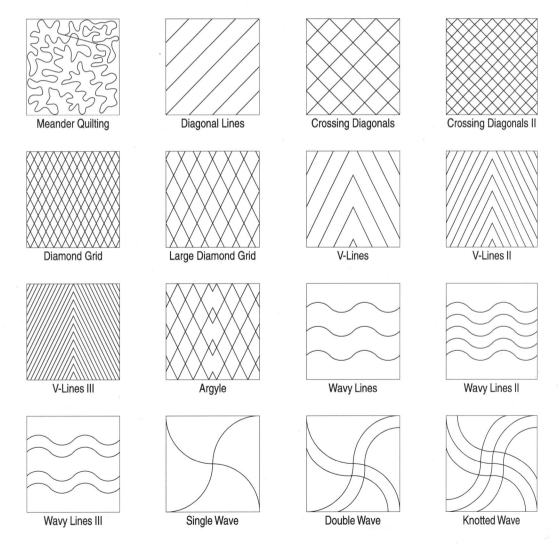

Meander Quilting	Diagonal Lines	Crossing Diagonals	Crossing Diagonals II
Diamond Grid	Large Diamond Grid	V-Lines	V-Lines II
V-Lines III	Argyle	Wavy Lines	Wavy Lines II
Wavy Lines III	Single Wave	Double Wave	Knotted Wave

Waving Grid

Scallops

Double Scallop

Wavy & Straight

Pumpkin Seeds

Pumpkin Seeds II

Pumpkin Seeds III

Clover

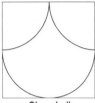
Clamshell

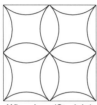
Wineglass (Straight)

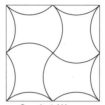
Seeds & Waves

 7 Quilting Stencils

 Wreaths

Rosebud Wreath

Sun Wreath

Interlocking Rings
Wreath

Flipped Feathers
Wreath

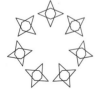
Simple Star Wreath

Starburst Wreath

Braid Wreath

Feather Wreath with
Heart

Heart Wreath   Heart Wreath 2   Heart Wreath 3   Heart Wreath 4

Sunflower Wreath   Sawtooth Wreath   Looped Ring Wreath   Circle Wreath

Petal Wreath   Petal Wreath 2   Feather Wreath   Feather Wreath 2

Feather Wreath 3   Feather Wreath 4   Simple Wreath

8 Overlaid Blocks

8 Overlaid Blocks

 Embellished Alphabet

A is for Apple

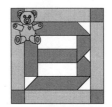

B is for Bear

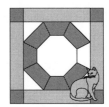

C is for Cat

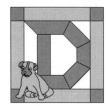

D is for Dog

E is for Egg

F is for Fish

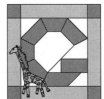

G is for Giraffe

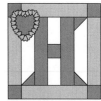

H is for Heart

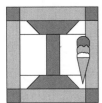

I is for Ice Cream
Cone

J is for
Jack-o'-Lantern

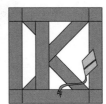

K is for Kite

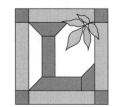

L is for Leaf

M is for Moon

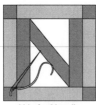

N is for Needle

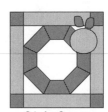

O is for Orange

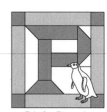

P is for Penguin

Q is for Queen

R is for Robot

S is for Snowflake

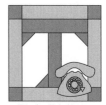

T is for Telephone

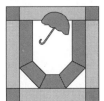

U is for Umbrella

V is for Violin

W is for Watering Can

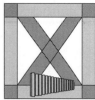

X is for Xylophone

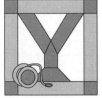

Y is for Yo Yo

Z is for Zebra

8 Overlaid Blocks
Fancy Flowers

Striped Floral

Petal Snowflake

Orange Blossom

Bluebell Star

Overlapping Hearts

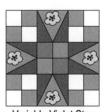

Variable Violet Star

Violet Star Bouquet

Andrea's Fancy

Whirling Buds &
Berries

Purple Petals

Rotate Surprise

Flowering Ohio Star

Flowering Wheel

Rising Waves

Valentine Album

Flower-in-the-Box

Fall Dance

Trellis

9-Patch Flower

Stained-Glass Window

Scattered Leaves

Blooming Orchid

Glass Sunflower

Spring Flowers

Shady Window

 8 Overlaid Blocks

Pictures

Fish Tank

May Basket

Mother's Day Basket

Laurel & Lyre

Key West

Sailor's Delight

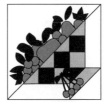

Fancy Fruit

Fall Flowers

Sunny Sail

First Bloom

Christmas Morning

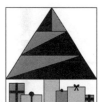

Presents Under the Tree

Evening Sail

Snowy Day

Barn Friends

On the Lookout

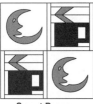

Sweet Dreams

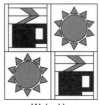

Wake Up

A Flock

Apple Tree

Sleep Tight

8 Overlaid Blocks

 Simple Designs

Patriotic Patch

Constellation Patch

Butterfly Star

Fantasia

Autumn Cross Patch

Framed Applique

Fan and Stars

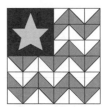

Stars and Stripes

Captured Feathers

Framed Stars

Star within Stars

Diamond Flower

Spiral Roses

Fanned Flowers

Flying Stars

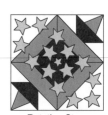

Rotating Stars

Now Showing

Spinning Snowflake

Woven Petals

Texas Wheel

Grapes of Wrath

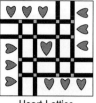

Heart Lattice

Index

C

C 9, 10, 132
c 132
C is for Cat 166
Cabbage Rose Wreath 101
Cabin 81
Cactus Bud 29
Cake 108
Cake Stand 35
Calico Cartoon Cat 107
Calico Puzzle 28
Camp, Coxey's 17
Candle 80, 111
Candle and Holder 111
Candle and Holly 111
Candy Canes 65, 110
Capital T 28
Captured Feathers 170
Car 127
Card Basket 31
Card Trick 29
Cardinal 113, 135
Carnation 139
Carnation (Rita Denenberg) 118
Carousel Horse (Rita Denenberg) 127
Carpie Fish 116, 137
Carrie Nation Quilt 26
Carrot 114, 142
Cartoon Cat Silhouette 107
Cat 50, 107
Cat Head 76
Cat Silhouette 145
Cats and Mice 30
Cat's Tails 57
CD 129
Celtic Circle 154
Celtic Hearts 120
Celtic Hearts with Leaves 120
Celtic Interweave 154
Celtic Patch 126
Celtic Patch (2) 126
Celtic Patch (3) 126
Celtic Patch (4) 126
Celtic Patch (5) 126
Celtic Patch (6) 126

Celtic Patch (7) 126
Celtic Rope 154
Celtic Squares and Loops 154
Celtic Squares and Loops (2) 154
Celtic Squares and Loops (3) 154
Center Diamond Variation 38
Ceramic Planter 74
Chain (1) 53
Chariot Wheel 16
Charm Basket 47
Check (1A) 13
Check (1B) 13
Check and Triangle (2) 43
Check and Triangle (3) 43
Check and Triangle (4) 43
Check and Triangle Border 43
Checked X 63
Checkerboard 41
Checkerboard Basket 47
Cherries 142
Cherry Wreath 103
Chet (Debbie Sichel) 79
Chevrons & Strips 43
Chevrons and Stripes 44
Cheyenne Star 59
Chicago 56
Chicago Star 27, 39
Chick (Rita Denenberg) 115
Children's Delight 24
China Doll (Rita Denenberg) 127
Chinese Lanterns 32
Chips and Whetstones 15
Chloe Fish 116, 137
Christ Child (Rita Denenberg) 112
Christmas Cactus 103
Christmas Goose 112
Christmas Morning 169
Christmas Pine 68
Christmas Snowflake 160
Christmas Stocking (Rita Denenberg) 112
Christmas Tree 80, 88, 111
Christmas Tree (Rita Denenberg) 111

Churn Dash 15
Circle Rose 95, 140
Circle Rose II 95
Circle Star 15, 16
Circle Wreath 163
Circle-in-a-Circle 155
Circle-in-a-Circle II 155
Clamshell 33, 155, 162
Clarinet (Rita Denenberg) 122
Classic Dresden Plate 19
Clay's Choice 14, 25
Cloud 114, 143
Clover 155, 162
Clown 24
Clown Doll 127
Clown's Choice 29
Cock's Comb 41
Cock's Comb and Currants 96
Coffin Star 17, 38
Collie 50
Colonial Girl 148
Colonial Lady 102
Comb 95
Comet 57
Coming Home (Rita Denenberg) 112
Comma 134
Compass Star 15
Computer Monitor 129
Computer Tower 129
Condo 57
Coneflower 140
Coneflower II 140
Constellation Patch 170
Continuous Line Bells 152
Continuous Line Double Ovals 152
Continuous Line Fall 152
Continuous Line Feathers 152
Continuous Line Fish 152
Continuous Line Flowers 152
Continuous Line Hearts 152
Continuous Line Houses 152
Continuous Line Maple Leaves 152
Continuous Line Moon & Stars 152

D